The Year of the Poet VIII

August 2021

The Poetry Posse

inner child press, ltd.

The Poetry Posse 2021

Gail Weston Shazor
Shareef Abdur Rasheed
Teresa E. Gallion
hülya n. yılmaz
Kimberly Burnham
Tzemin Ition Tsai
Elizabeth Esguerra Castillo
Jackie Davis Allen
Joe Paire
Caroline 'Ceri' Nazareno
Ashok K. Bhargava
Alicja Maria Kuberska
Swapna Behera
Albert 'Infinite' Carrasco
Eliza Segiet
William S. Peters, Sr.

~ * ~

In order to maintain each poet's authentic voice, this volume has not undergone the scrutiny of editing. Please take time to indulge each contributor for their own creativity and aspirations to convey their uniqueness.

hülya n. yılmaz, Ph.D.
Director of Editing ~
Inner Child Press International

General Information

The Year of the Poet VIII
August 2021 Edition

The Poetry Posse

1st Edition : 2021

This Publishing is protected under Copyright Law as a "Collection". All rights for all submissions are retained by the Individual Author and or Artist. No part of this Publishing may be Reproduced, Transferred in any manner without the prior **WRITTEN CONSENT** of the "Material Owners" or its Representative Inner Child Press. Any such violation infringes upon the Creative and Intellectual Property of the Owner pursuant to International and Federal Copyright Laws. Any queries pertaining to this "Collection" should be addressed to Publisher of Record.

Publisher Information
1st Edition : Inner Child Press
intouch@innerchildpress.com
www.innerchildpress.com

This Collection is protected under U.S. and International Copyright Laws

Copyright © 2021 : The Poetry Posse

ISBN-13 : 978-1-952081-53-8 (inner child press, ltd.)

$ 12.99

WHAT WOULD LIFE BE WITHOUT A LITTLE POETRY?

Dedication

This Book is dedicated to

Humanity, Peace & Poetry

the Power of the Pen
can effectuate change!

&

The Poetry Posse

past, present & future
our Patrons and Readers
the Spirit of our Everlasting Muse

*In the darkness of my life
I heard the music
I danced...
and the Light appeared
and I dance*

Janet P. Caldwell

Table of Contents

Foreword — ix
Preface — xii
The Feature : Mundara Koorang — xv

The Poetry Posse

Gail Weston Shazor	1
Alicja Maria Kuberska	9
Jackie Davis Allen	15
Tezmin Ition Tsai	23
Shareef Abdur – Rasheed	29
Kimberly Burnham	37
Elizabeth Esguerra Castillo	43
Joe Paire	49
hülya n. yılmaz	55
Teresa E. Gallion	61
Ashok K. Bhargava	67
Caroline Nazareno-Gabis	73

Table of Contents . . . *continued*

Swapna Behera — 79
Albert Carassco — 87
Eliza Segiet — 93
William S. Peters, Sr. — 99

August Featured Poets — 109

Caroline Laurent Turunc — 111
Kamal Dhungana — 121
Pankhuri Sinha — 129
Paramita Mukherjee Mullick — 139

Inner Child News — 149
Other Anthological Works — 181

Foreword

"We are all visitors to this time ,this place, we are just passing through .
Our purpose here is to observe ,to learn, to grow, to love and then we return home."

Australian aboriginal proverb .

The Year of the Poet has taken ekphrastic poetry for 2021 ; reflecting the world famous pictures of our time. The word ekphrasis, or ecphrasis, comes from the Greek for the written description of a work of art produced as a rhetorical exercise, often used in the adjectival form ekphrastic. It is the verbal description of a visual work of art, either real or imagined. Any poem about art, whether rhymed or unrhymed, metrical or free verse, may be considered ekphrastic .

In August our theme is on the painting of Mundara Koorang .

Mundara Koorang is an Australian Aboriginal artist, designer, teacher, elder, actor, and author.He was born in 1952 in the Eora (Sydney) New South Wales and is descendant of the Gamilaroi people. Mundara's grandmother, great grandmother and great-great grandmother were all born in the Barwon River , Brewarrina area. He is an internationally renowned Aboriginal artist and the recipient of the David O'Chin Photographic Award .His primary passion is the successful education of aboriginal people and he is a mentor of Indigenous people. He strongly believes that the indigenous people can and must be in control of their destinies.

In 2005 Mundara published a Dreamtime story entitled The Little Platypus and the Fire Spirit. Aboriginal Australians are the various Indigenous peoples of the Australian mainland and many of its islands, such as Tasmania, Fraser Island, .They love Nature . Symbols are used by Aboriginal people in their art to preserve their culture and tradition. They are also used to depict various stories and are still used today in contemporary Aboriginal Art.

White is the spirit colour. Black is the colour of night and represents Aboriginal people . Red is the colour of the land or of blood. Yellow is the colour of the sun and sacred.

There are several types of and methods used in making Aboriginal art, including rock painting, dot painting, rock engravings, bark painting, carvings, sculptures, and weaving and string art. Australian Aboriginal art is the oldest unbroken tradition of art in the world.

The Inner Child Press with its mission of building bridges of cultural understanding takes the responsibility for global peace and harmony through poetry with International Anthologies.

We respect the land ,nature, folk tales, culture, music, literature ,perceptions, ideas, thoughts ,language, art, artisans and all ethnic groups of the world

Literature has undergone a tectonic change .

We express our deep reverence to all for they are the apostles of a time zone who have solved the situations, saved human lives and helped the economic, cultural social growth of society .

Painting is poetry of Nature. Poetry is the living song of human race ....

We respect the humanity ...
We respect history and coexistence

Let us join our hands for peace and build a paradise on the Earth ...

Swapna Behera
Cultural Ambassador of India and south East Asia for Inner Child Press International

Preface

Dear Family and Friends,

So, here we are, now in our 8th month of our eighth year of monthly publication of *The Year of the Poet*. Amazing how much effort has been given by all the poets, to include the various members of *The Poetry Posse* and all the wonderful featured poets from all over our world. For myself, it has been and continues to be a great honor to be a part of this wonderful cooperative effort.

Last year, 2020 has been challenging for many of us throughout the year. We at *Inner Child Press International* were busy. We envisioned our role where the arts meet humanity to continue doing what we were good at . . . publishing. We managed to not only produce and publish this series, *The Year of the Poet* each month, but we were also very proactive in the arena of human and social consciousness. We were able to produce several other anthologies to include: World Healing, World Peace 2020; CORONA . . . social distancing; The Heart of a Poet; W.A.R. . . we are revolution; Poetry, the Best of 2020. Going forward, we are seeking to invest in the same or greater effort towards contributing to a 'conscious humanity'. We, poets and writers do have something to say about it all, and we intend to do so in any and every way we can. So stay tuned . . .

Bill

William S. Peters, Sr.

Publisher
Inner Child Press International

www.innerchildpress.com

PS

Do Not forget about the World Healing, World Peace Poetry initiative for 2022. Mark your calendars. Submissions will be opening . . .
September 1st 2021

Past volumes are vailable here

www.worldhealingworldpeacepoetry.com

For Free Downloads of Previous Issues of The Year of the Poet

www.innerchildpress.com/the-year-of-the-poet

Mundara Koorang

August 2021

Mundara Koorang's grandmother, great grandmother and great-great grandmother were all born in the Barwon River, Brewarrina area of Australia. Koorang also known as Thunder Snake is an Australian Aboriginal artist, designer, teacher, elder, actor, and author. A descendant of the Gamilaroi people, Koorang was born in 1952 in the Eora (Sydney) of Australia's NSW area. A firm believer that indigenous people can and must be in control of their own destinies, one of his primary passions is the successful education of Aboriginal people. Mundara teaches at a TAFE campus, Year 10 Community school for children who can't or won't attend school and at a Juvenile Justice centre of boys who have ended up on the wrong side of the law. He teaches Literacy & Numeracy, Art, Drawing, Legislation, Mathematics, Science, History, Cultural practices, Perspectives and Kinship, and is a Mentor for young indigenous people.

http://koorang.auctivacommerce.com/
http://mundara.com.au

The Little Platypus and the Fire Spirit written and illustrated by Mundara Koorang "A long time ago in the Dreamtime there was a little animal called a platypus. He was not as we know him today. The platypus lived in the bush. He had a long skinny tail and long ears. His fur was brown and he loved to run through the bush chasing bugs and butterflies ..."

Mundara Koorang

Poets . . .
sowing seeds in the
Conscious Garden of Life,
that those who have yet to come
may enjoy the Flowers.

Poets, Writers . . . know that we are the enchanting magicians that nourishes the seeds of dreams and thoughts . . . it is our words that entice the hearts and minds of others to believe there is something grand about the possibilities that life has to offer and our words tease it forth into action . . . for you are the Poet, the Writer to whom the Gift of Words has been entrusted . . .

~ wsp

Poetry is . . .

Poetry succeeds where instruction fails.

~ wsp

Gail Weston Shazor

Gail Weston Shazor

This is a creative promise ~ my pen will speak to and for the world. Enamored with letters and respectful of their power, I have been writing for most of my life. A mother, daughter, sister and grandmother I give what I have been given, greatfilledly.

Author of . . .

"An Overstanding of an Imperfect Love"
&
Notes from the Blue Roof

Lies My Grandfathers Told Me

available at Inner Child Press.

www.facebook.com/gailwestonshazor
www.innerchildpress.com/gail-weston-shazor
navypoet1@gmail.com

Snakes

Cold
Coiling
Clever
Cerulean flashed with red
Climbing
Closer
Ceilings
Cabled glimmerings
Calligraphy
Casing
Cabobs
Causing flourishes

On my totem

A Prayer

It is in this moment Abba Father
That the road seems to have grown
A might bit long, Lord
And the task hard to complete
Weariness overtakes the evening
And it is with the heaviness
Of a battle scarred soldier
That the pillow beckons a head
But it is not the flesh that requires
A long respite
Only A flagging spirit in need of
Recharging
You know every need
That is lacking
And it only require a request
Fueled with repentance and faith
For imminent renewal
This broken offering is ready
To be made ready
For another day...
Greatfilledly

Mississippi

I can never tally all that you gave me
The lives that live on in my laughter, in my tears
Those who have come and gone before
Memories that bring both joy and pain
Fish fries and coconut cakes and on each
Fourth Sunday, humming jones greeting
Those headed out to meet up with Jesus
At Provident Baptist Church
Of my dear papaw who carried my spirit
Inside his Prince Albert can close to his right hand
Side pocket of Sunday's best striped overalls
That we bought on our annual trip to Webb
Off route 49 and 32, after a trip to visit
The Cascilla cousins on his side of the family
Of mama who rose up early just to make
The G biscuit and coffee and cream
Who let me pack my papaw's lunch
And sold moonshine, regulating with
A 22 piece stashed in her apron pocket
Who everyone called ma'am, even us kids
Love covered the feet of granddaddy snow
As he searched through Charleston General
With the fear that I couldn't be found
Though I slept with the white babies, snug and sound
Who ran a jook joint on Saturday nights so the
Black folks could let their hair down after
Hot days of working in the cotton fields
And Pearl, who folks say I look like and act like
With my plain spoken, straight ways, nosey always
Searching for something more than what life has to offer
Wearing pants in town, around the courthouse square and
Down by the piggly wiggly, sunflower and the chinaman's

Uptown, trading with the folks, summer peaches and gossip
Fresh and ripe as the sun on the back of her hatless head
The neighbors, family and friends, them white folks and some
That was neither and both depending on who you ask
Fields plowed long and straight waiting on seed
Fireplaces and slop jars, rifles and aprons, gavels and gloves
Front porches that stretched round and covered the edges
Of your heart, soul and spirit cool in the evening and a place
For shelling purple hull peas, snapping beans and listening to stories
Getting your hair combed after Saturday baths in the foot tub
You, who have been have been my constant companion
When I talk with my mother, my father, uncles and aunts
I am back walking down the street, chewing bubble gum
And seeing the familiar faces who knew me always as
T and Snow's granddaughter and so and so's cousin
You are my memory bearer, life cradle, my bone keeper
Even now, when I turn right off 55 and head down 32
And the blacktop is shimmering with heat like smoke
Whether in car or mind, I am so much closer to being home.

Gail Weston Shazor

Alicja Maria Kuberska

Alicja Maria Kuberska

Alicja Maria Kuberska – awarded Polish poetess, novelist, journalist, editor.

She is a member of the Polish Writers Associations in Warsaw, Poland and IWA Bogdani, Albania. She is also a member of directors' board of Soflay Literature Foundation, Our Poetry Archive (India) and Cultural Ambassador for Poland (Inner Child Press, USA)

Her poems have been published in numerous anthologies and magazines in : Poland, Czech Republic, Slovakia, Hungary,Ukraina, Belgium, Bulgaria, Albania, Spain, the UK, Italy, the USA, Canada, the UK, Argentina, Chile, Peru, Israel, Turkey, India, Uzbekistan, South Korea, Taiwan, China, Australia, South Africa, Zambia, Nigeria

She received two medals - the Nosside UNESCO Competition in Italy (2015) and European Academy of Science Arts and Letters in France (2017). Ahe also received a reward of international literary competition in Italy „ Tra le parole e 'elfinito" (2018). She was announced a poet of the 2017 year by Soflay Literature Foundation (2018).She also received : Bolesław Prus Prize Poland (2019), Culture Animator Poland (2019) and first prize Premio Internazionale di Poesia Poseidonia- Paestrum Italy (2019).

Dreamtime

In the stories of old men
like the boomerang
stories about the past and memories
describing the dream time return

On a path made of words
past meets present time,
ancient animals come to life
and again platypus runs
 through the bush in pursuit of butterflies,
and the Fire Spirit dances in the grass.

Modern art draws from tradition
and it does not let forget
about Aboriginal roots
The images are intertwined
with themes from the rock carvings

Smell

Violet, tiny flower,
where did you hide ?
I wish I knew
where you got such a beautiful color,
a wonderful scent.
In vain I am looking for you
among the slender lilies
and elegant roses.
I look for you in the violet of irises.

The wind revealed the secret.
You hid among the tall grass
and you hugged modest daisies.

You soared together with the larks
straight to heaven
on subtle notes of aroma.

Violets and Roses

Violet
-the hero of sentimental entries
in a girl's diary
Today
it is still a violet drop of blood
of eternal friendship,
sealed with dried petals.

Rose
-the flower of love
even after death
it stores a subtle scent of past moments
in dried petals,
but the touch crushes memories

Jackie Davis Allen

Jackie Davis Allen

Jackie Davis Allen, otherwise known as Jacqueline D. Allen or Jackie Allen, grew up in the Cumberland Mountains of Appalachia. As the next eldest daughter of a coal miner father and a stay at home mother, she was the first in her family to attend and graduate from college. Her siblings, in their own right, are accomplished, though she is the only one, to date, that has discovered the gift of writing.

Graduating from Radford University, with a Bachelors of Science degree in Early Education, she taught in both public and private schools. For over a decade she taught private art classes to children both in her home and at a local Art and Framing Shop where she also sold her original soft sculptured Victorian dolls and original christening gowns.

She resides in northern Virginia with her husband, taking much needed get-aways to their mountain home near the Blue Ridge Mountains, a place that evokes memories of days spent growing up in the Appalachian Mountains.

A lover of hats, she has worn many. Following marriage to her college sweetheart, and as wife, mother, grandmother, teacher, tutor, artist, writer, poet and crafter, she is a lover of art and antiques, surrounding herself, always, with books, seeking to learn more.

In 2015 she authored *Looking for Rainbows, Poetry, Prose and Art*, and in 2017, *Dark Side of the Moon*. Both books of mostly narrative poetry were published by Inner Child Press and were edited by hulya n. yilmaz.

in 2019, No Illusions.Through the Looking Glass, which was nominated to be considered for a Pulitzer Prize by the publisher and editor of InnerChild Press, ltd.

http://www.innerchildpress.com/jackie-davis-allen.php
jackiedavisallen.com

Hauntingly Designed

Across the ocean.
Beneath the clouds.
Looking inward, outward.

Haunting.

Looms the past, the present,
Ever always, images of a river flowing.
Filled with history, family, passion, art.

Design.

The drumbeat of the land
Hot, cold, heart-painted, passionate.
Spirit-filled-colors frame the canvas. Pigmented.

Hauntingly.

Originality coils, snakes
Like a ancient river. Prepared
It forcefully flows, springs forth.

Designed.

Traversed

Like the highest
Of mountains climbed
Or the deepest waters forged,
Yours, mine.
Ours is a friendship wrought
From traversing, together
Poetry and prose.
How has the grace
Of time passed,
Treasured, valued,
Unsurpassed. Sublime.
Our finest wines
Poured out, freely
East to west,
West to east:
Both ways.
Mutual respect lingers
Along with admiration.
Ours, a friendship
Like poetic second skin.
Friend to friend.

Jackie Davis Allen

A Poet's Rose

At the introspective age
Of forty four or forty five,
Maria heard the beckoning call
Of "Self-discovery."

Like a greedy little child,
Innocent, with conscious
Remaining virginally mute,
She abandoned all caution.

And hastily, flying away,
Left all behind.
Desperate in the hope
Of finding a special identity.

Above and beyond
The rugged mountain tops,
High on turbulent clouds
Of euphoria, Maria soared.

Intoxicated, inebriated,
Crisscrossing dark holes,
Weight of responsibility suddenly
Clipped her uncertain wings.

Hesitating, despondent, yet
With resolve, determination won;
And our sweet Maria's fragrance
Succumbed like a faded rose.

On recrimination's knees, filled
with remorse, she prayed for relief.
Then, profusely, accepting pardon,
She reached out with gladness.

In the expansive garden of self
Maria tilled deeply its soil,
And there found growing, her voice
As intoxicatingly-perfumed as any rose.

Jackie Davis Allen

Tzemin Ition Tsai

Tzemin Ition Tsai

Dr. Tzemin Ition Tsai (□ □ □ □ □) was born in Republic of China, in 1957. He holds a Ph.D. in Chemical Engineering and two Masters of Science in Applied Mathematics and Chemical Engineering. He is a professor at Asia University (Taiwan), editor of "Reading, Writing and Teaching" academic text. He also writes the long-term columns for Chinese Language Monthly in Taiwan.

He is a scholar with a wide range of expertise, while maintaining a common and positive interest in science, engineering and literature member. He is also an editor of "Reading, Writing and Teaching" academic text and a columnist for *'Chinese Language Monthly'* in Taiwan

He has won many national literary awards. His literary works have been anthologized and published in books, journals, and newspapers in more than 40 countries and have been translated into more than a dozen languages.

A gift from the wind

Just at noon
TV keeps telling news of typhoon
The terrible "Through-heart Typhoon" with a 13-level wind
I can't help but tremble
The next day, that call by grandmother
The roof of my old home was gone
A few days later
With mom and dad
Lying on the bed that was over a hundred years old
We all were looking at the sky
In addition to the wall of mud bricks around
The original roof was empty
A surprise never felt before
Endless sky
Full of stars
The whole family were busy counting the countless flashes
completely forgot
We were
The victims of Typhoon MEGI

The ants are so happy

Mommy Mommy
Birthday today
Go nowhere
Just lie in the yard
Daddy cut a plate of big pears
Want me to take it to mommy
My little hand is not strong enough
Dropped the pears all over the floor

Mommy is not angry at all
Touching my hair and is still smiling
Oh, my little baby
You don't need to worry
Bring the rest to Mommy
Let the rest lying on the ground be there in a moment
We will very quickly have a group of
Joyous ants

Grandpa's loofah shed

The row of camphor trees beside the house
The year I was born
Grandpa planted it by hand
Has grown up like me
Green branches and leaves stretch around
Interconnected in a circle
summer
When the sun hangs high in the sky
Spitting out air is like coming from a stove
Grandpa set up a loofah shed
Under the only cool shade
On the one hand you can enjoy the cool
On the one hand waiting for the harvest
When he lies under the loofah shed
Looking at the loofahs one by one
He will smile to me
Those naughty loofahs
Very much like
you of
a little child who has not grown up

Shareef Abdur Rasheed

Shareef Abdur Rasheed

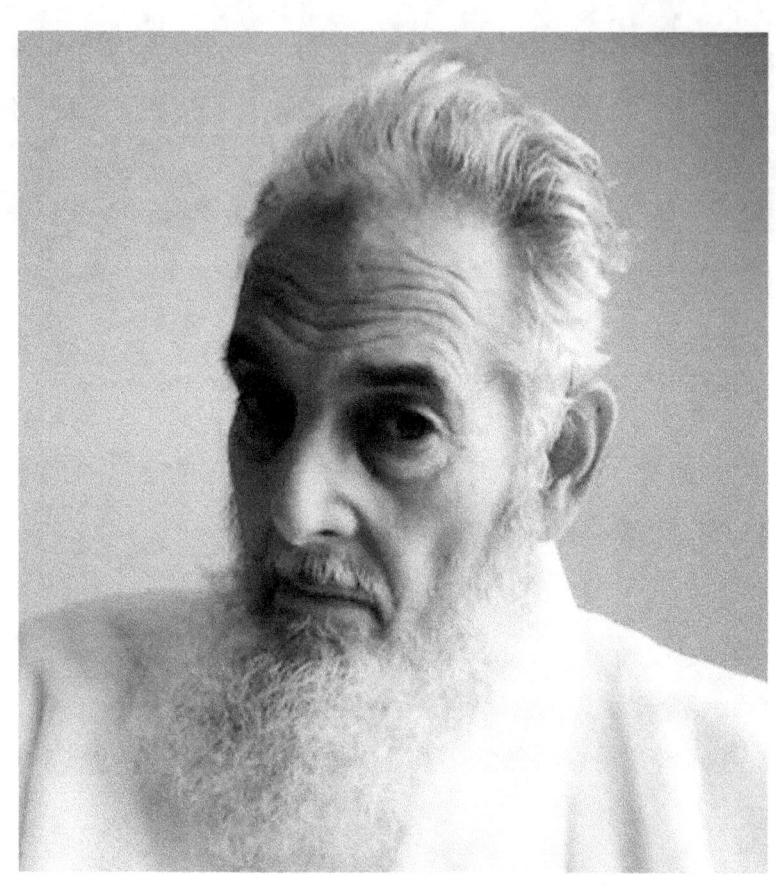

Shareef Abdur-Rasheed, AKA Zakir Flo was born and raised in Brooklyn, New York. His education includes Brooklyn College, Suffolk County Community College and Makkah, Saudi Arabia. He is a Veteran of the Viet Nam era, where in 1969 he reverted to his now reverently embraced Islamic Faith. He is very active in the Islamic community and beyond with his teachings, activism and his humanity.

Shareef's spiritual expression comes through the persona of "Zakir Flo" . Zakir is Arabic for "To remind". Never silent, Shareef Abdur-Rasheed is always dropping science, love, consciousness and signs of the time in rhyme.

Shareef is the Patriarch of the Abdur-Rasheed Family with 9 Children (6 Sons and 3 Daughters) and 41 Grandchildren (24 Boys and 17 Girls).

For more information about Shareef, visit his personal FaceBook Page at :

https://www.facebook.com/shareef.abdurrasheed1
https://zakirflo.wordpress.com

Mentor Mundara Koorang

indigenous, aboriginal artist
from eora- sydney people
elder, multi talented
in his artwork reflecting
aboriginal cultural influence
patterns, colors, shapes, figures
his gifts shared with his people
as a actor included young
aboriginal youth in his films
exposing them to the world
of film making
activist from strong roots
always lifting up his people
who have been brutalized by a
racist, supremist regime for many
years as to be controlled, marginalized
deprived of rights that are reserved
only for so called white Australians of
European descent
his art extends to photography writing,
educating aboriginal cultural ethics
and perspectives
a gem in the aboriginal community this
multi talented humanitarian.

race no race

oh mankind
made you into tribes and nations
said the lord
cee?
heed word of the lord
cee?
that you may know one another
not despise one another
that you may know one another
not despise one another
it may come as a suprise
race no race only nations, tribes
this how mankind is comprised
the best of you are the most
devoted to me
said the lord
listen people to the wahi
cee?
revelation it means
describing true history
humanbeings
who better could describe origin
of humanity then he who created
you and me
no mention of race not so much as a trace
the big lie falls on it's face as it's designer
disgraced yes this lie the devil creates
Race No Race, Race No Race, Race No Race
Big lie to divide this word to be despised
has come in disguise as a fact
but this a lie to be attacked, sent back
to the one who comes from the back

Shareef Abdur Rasheed

to lead mankind astray
take truth away
oh mankind i made you into tribes and
nations
to know one another not despise
one another
beauty in diversity, identity all tribes, nations
all mankind
but remember the best of you are most devoted
have you heard this,
Race No Race, Race No Race.

Demanded in full

fits like this
foot in shoe
do what you must do
to restore truth
justice due
trust truth through
testing you
see what you do
when hardship hits you
revealing real you
exposing fake posing
no suprise how creame
rise to the top
disguise stops
when giving the trust
to do what you must
pick up the slack for the
rest of us
cast in the roll to be the one
to make folks whole
like restitution pays what's
owed.
then y'all know how justice flo
so don't trip on the glow,
glitter that Shaitan throws
as the saying goes
" all that glitter ain't gold "
y'all stop, listen up that's
truth, justice rising to the top.

Shareef Abdur Rasheed

Kimberly Burnham

Kimberly Burnham

A brain health expert with a PhD in Integrative Medicine, Kimberly Burnham has lived in tropical Colombia; in Belgium during the Vietnam War; in Japan teaching businessmen English; in diverse international Toronto, Canada; and several places in the US. Now, she's in Spokane, WA with her wife, Elizabeth, two sets of twins (age 11 & 14) and three dogs. Her recent book, *Awakenings: Peace Dictionary, Language and the Mind, a Daily Brain Health Program* includes the word for peace in hundreds of languages. Her poetry weaves through 80+ volumes of *The Year of the Poet, Inspired by Gandhi, Women Building the World*, and *A Woman's Place in the Dictionary*. She is currently working on several ekphrastic writing projects. One is a novel, *Art Thief Cracks Healing Code for Parkinson's Disease* and the other is non-fiction, *Using Ekphrastic Fiction Writing and Poetry to Create Interest and Promote Artists, Writers, and Poets*.

http://www.NerveWhisperer.Solutions

https://healthy-brain.medium.com/bears-at-the-window-of-climate-change-d1fb403eeaf3

Golden Light

Creative color from within

the center of a conscious mind

blue legs ready

a taut body swift

on a sea of red

traveling a golden path

in through the viewer's eyes

touching consciousness

lighting the spark anew

amid red and blue spirals

Symbols of Life Creating Reality

A snake, a turtle, and a kangaroo

hop into a painting

out of a man's intellect

life is no joke

where symbols abound

Well Fed on Peace

What are we well fed on
what emotion or state of being
comes most often
in Warlpiri, an indigenous language of Australia
"iawa-nyinami" means peace
and "jantukula" is peaceful
"pukurlpa" suggests many things
peace, happy, content, satisfied,
and well fed
all nuances of one word
while "kalypapayi" describes a way to be
habitually at peace
one like me
who prefers not to fight

Elizabeth E. Castillo

Elizabeth Esguerra Castillo

Elizabeth Esguerra Castillo is a multi-awarded and an Internationally-Published Contemporary Author/Poet and a Professional Writer / Creative Writer / Feature Writer / Journalist / Travel Writer from the Philippines. She has 2 published books, "Seasons of Emotions" (UK) and "Inner Reflections of the Muse", (USA). Elizabeth is also a co-author to more than 60 international anthologies in the USA, Canada, UK, Romania, India. She is a Contributing Editor of Inner Child Magazine, USA and an Advisory Board Member of Reflection Magazine, an international literary magazine. She is a member of the American Authors Association (AAA) and PEN International.

Web links:

Facebook Fan Page

https://free.facebook.com/ElizabethEsguerraCastillo

Google Plus

https://plus.google.com/u/0/+ElizabethCastillo

Elizabeth Esguerra Castillo

Dream to Be Free

He dreamt of becoming free

From a world which casts him out

A free spirit, he was a captive

Pleading for mercy

He dreamt of running free

To live in another lifetime

Where he truly belongs.

Canvass

The arid air smells of melancholy
Like a ship wrecked, out of direction
Sailing against the tide
Fighting the ebb and flow of life
I hear your voice from a distance
But suddenly, I was awakened
And realized it was just a memory
A memory of your serene face
Your kind eyes, your sweet gaze
That look of innocence.

Field of Memories

In a frenzy,
Engulfed in oblivion
Sinking deep
In the abyss of memories
Of yesteryears
Seeking you
In every person I meet
Field of memories
Fragments of time
Enveloped by dreams of forever.

Joe Paire

Joe Paire

Joseph L Paire' aka Joe DaVerbal Minddancer . . .
is a quiet man, born in a time where civil liberties were a walk on thin ice. He's been a victim of his own shyness often sidelined in his own quest for love. He became the observer, charting life's path. Taking note of the why, people do what they do. His writings oft times strike a cord with the dormant strings of the reader. His pen the rosined bow drawn across the mind. He comes full-frontal or in the subtlest way, always expressing in a way that stimulate the senses.

www.facebook.com/joe.minddancer

Joe Paire

What A Beautiful Tapestry

Where do I display such a lovely art piece?
Which wall could hold the space?
Where grubby hands are free?

I can't afford the loss of space,
Nor do I have room for an altar.
I remember plastic covered furniture
That never got sat on by the elders.

I can see the artists vision,
Mundara Koorang, I believe his name is.
What I can't see is beyond the borders of a tapestry.

An aboriginal original dedicated to teaching youths.
But the borders of circles in yellow, purple and blues.
You interpret for you; I interpret the hues.
I've found the perfect spot for my tapestry
in the center of my room.

Time Space Continuum

I've watched them grow from tot to old.
Nothing ever changes but time.
I've made a few notches in this world tho cold
I still haven't made up my mind.

Sound travels, light travels, life exists in experiments
Where's the formular for normal behavior.
Are we really ever near to it?

Am I scared of it; I don't fit any molds "mind made"?
Human life share the studies of some animals.
Some folk act like we're still in caves.

I don't do structure well.
While some folks adhere to timelines.
If my calculations are right,
I've held on to a young mind.

Everything ages from the second it's born.
I've watched children grow to have children.
If it's so basic to procreate, do we regulate who shouldn't?

Time space continuum, how can we continue them.
The changes, Those choices, the infamous voices
The voice of the voiceless, even the worst of us.
Cling to a prescribed life, but not I.

Everything is new to me, and everything gets old
I can only be true to me; the rest gets stories told.

Summer Ends

The warm weather feels good.
They say it's okay to mingle.
Company came by to just say hi.
I say, it was nice to see you.

It's not the same anymore
As the leaves are turning quickly.
Masks are more or less a fashion statement
The whole world seems so sickly.

Two people got stung with summer fun
One by wasp, one by bee.
I sprayed the nest with a power shot
But nature is always free.

Clumps of green are turning brown
And orchids are falling and eaten
I saw a deer across the road
On orange blossoms she was feasting.

Three grills for free meals,
the take home crew is here.
They'll feed their children for the following week
And drink up all my beer.

School is going to start again,
with the air not sure or certain.
Summer ends as the flu begins.
Another bout could mean curtains.

hülya n. yılmaz

hülya n. yılmaz

Professor Emerita (Humanities, Penn State, USA), hülya n. yılmaz [sic] is a published tri-lingual author, literary translator, and Director of Editing Services (Inner Child Press International, USA). Her work has appeared in numerous anthologies of global endeavors and was presented at poetry events in the U.S. and abroad. In 2018, the WIN of British Colombia, Canada honored yılmaz with a literary excellence award. Her two poems remain permanently installed in *Telepoem Booth* (USA). hülya finds it vital for everyone to understand a deeper sense of self, and writes creatively to attain a comprehensive awareness for and development of our humanity.

Writing Web Site
https://hulyanyilmaz.com/

Editing Web Site
https://hulyasfreelancing.com

hülya n. yılmaz

A Poem Trilogy to Honor Mundara Koorang

Thunder Snake

1952.
The Eora.
Australia,
the birthplace of and home to
approximately 864,200 aboriginal peoples.
Mundara Koorang is born.
The snake is his totem.

Years later,
his is a prominent name.
Thunder Snake . . .

develops into an artist, actor, author,
a designer and a teacher.
He sates a primary passion
through his dedication to education.
Furthermore, he is committed to mentoring
troubled or underprivileged youth.
He spreads his consciousness of the dire necessity
to control one's own destiny.

In and beyond the Eora of Australia,
Indigenous people begin to take possession
of their own destinies.
Literacy is no longer
one of the unattainable luxuries.

The Gamilaroi

I imagine a river
where all my ancestors were born.
I imagine a river
which I can visit time and time again.
I imagine a river
where the living and the deceased conjoin
as kin spirits, as united energies.

River Barwon is that place for this trilogy's Honoree.

I imagine Thunder Snake
who was born to the Gamilaroi.
I imagine the banks of Barwon
in the Brewarrina Shire.
I imagine he is reunited there
with all his ancestors in spirit.
I imagine that historically distinguished area
of Australia where each of them began their life.

I imagine being at River Barwon.

I imagine sensing the energies of the Honoree's deceased.

I imagine meeting Thunder Snake in person.

I imagine attending one of his courses.

I imagine him teaching me
how to take control of my own destiny.

I am, after all, also a person
who exists in the third space . . . culturally.

"Dreamtime"

Come!
Come one, come all!
Whether you are a child or an adult,
come and witness the visual and writing artistry
of Mundara Koorang, today's Honoree!
If nothing else, please take a look at
The Little Platypus and the Fire Spirit,
a critically acclaimed children's book.
Come and enjoy his own illustrations,
among other small and big written beauties.

Come!
Come one, come all!
Take a magical and informative trip
to the "Dreamtime" along the "Dreamtime".
No matter what's our age,
we all are in dire need for a fantasy.

Teresa E. Gallion

Teresa E. Gallion

Teresa E. Gallion was born in Shreveport, Louisiana and moved to Illinois at the age of 15. She completed her undergraduate training at the University of Illinois Chicago and received her master's degree in Psychology from Bowling Green State University in Ohio. She retired from New Mexico state government in 2012.

She moved to New Mexico in 1987. While writing sporadically for many years, in 1998 she started reading her work in the local Albuquerque poetry community. She has been a featured reader at local coffee houses, bookstores, art galleries, museums, libraries, Outpost Performance Space, the Route 66 Festival in 2001 and the State of Oklahoma's Poetry Festival in Cheyenne, Oklahoma in 2004. She occasionally hosts an open mic.

Teresa's work is published in numerous Journals and anthologies. She has two CDs: *On the Wings of the Wind* and *Poems from Chasing Light*. She has published three books: *Walking Sacred Ground, Contemplation in the High Desert* and *Chasing Light.*

Chasing Light was a finalist in the 2013 New Mexico/Arizona Book Awards.

The surreal high desert landscape and her personal spiritual journey influence the writing of this Albuquerque poet. When she is not writing, she is committed to hiking the enchanted landscapes of New Mexico. You may preview her work at

http://bit.ly/1aIVPNq or *http://bit.ly/13IMLGh*

Platypus Dream

She dreams of the Platypus every night
running through the meadow next to the farm.
One night she decides to follow it
in the tall grasses glowing under the starlight.

Suddenly she stops and spiritual fire
surrounds the meadow.
She hears a tender voice speak in her head.

It is your time. Go forth and savor
the ecstatic beauty of planet earth.
Time is running out for destructive humans.
Kiss the earth with love before you leave
for the heavenly planes.

She awakens to mornings light
with a glowing smile on her face.

Fire Ring

I draw a circle around the fire ring
with my faithful hiking pole
and bow my head low
before the sacred purple moon.

Gratitude rushes through my veins.
The swell of peace surrounds my heart.
I am blessed with a spiritual moon.

Forgiveness washes my bones clean.
I glow before the night fire.
My soul is awakened to listen.

Distant memories linger as water ripples
massage my ears with songs
of peace, joy and love.

Solitude enfolds me like a warm blanket
sitting by the creek of reflection.
My tears sing back the joy
I feel from the water singing my name.

Teresa E. Gallion

Following My Tears

I smell my tears in the darkness.
No one told me fear brings blindness.
I must release fear
and open my eyes in the dark
to reach the easy pathway.

I follow the scent of my tears.
Light overtakes my body,
makes me adjust my eyes.
I see for the first time in the dark void
life floating pass me like a river's flow.

I can choose to step in anytime
readiness tickles my feet to move.
It is the sweet scent of my tears
that sustain me.
A special gift of love from Spirit.

Ashok K. Bhargava

Ashok K. Bhargava

Ashok Bhargava is a poet, writer, community activist, public speaker, management consultant and a keen photographer. Based in Vancouver, he has published several collections of his poems: Riding the Tide, Mirror of Dreams, A Kernel of Truth, Skipping Stones, Half Open Door and Lost in the Morning Calm. His poetry has been published in various literary magazines and anthologies.

Ashok is a Poet Laureate and poet ambassador to Japan, Korea and India. He is founder of WIN: Writers International Network Canada. Its main objective is to inspire, encourage, promote and recognize writers of diverse genres, artists and community leaders. He has received many accolades including Nehru Humanitarian Award for his leadership of Writers International Network Canada, Poets without Borders Peace Award for his journeys across the globe to celebrate peace and to create alliances with poets, and Kalidasa Award for creative writings.

Full Circle
For Mundara Koorang

Like a flute player charming a snake
let people feel the weight
of who you are and
let them deal with it.

In the meantime
like a cloud in blue sky
you keep on moving
forward with your passions.

Gracefully
unfold your layered heart
spread wings wide
soar like an eagle.

Sprinkle the heavens
with rainbow of colors
blue, azure and come back
full circle to the earth.

Soft Touch

If you wish to love me
then accept me as I am
and nothing else.

If you like to trust me
then believe in me
for no reason at all.

If you want to caress me
then touch me with your eyes
without asking why?

Because one day
my love will spring,
my passion will emerge,
my heart will blossom, and
my zeal will grow
for you.

But if you cannot wait for me
then without any hesitation
leave me and go away.
Because I can create you
when I am ready.

Beauty Lies Within Us

You can find meaning of life
only if you create it.

It is not lying out there
somewhere to be discovered.

It is within you
to bring it out and create it.

It is there like words for a poem
and tunes for a song.

It is up to you to compose a poem,
to sing a song to give a meaning to life.

Melody of a song, beauty of our deeds,
meaning of our life lies within us.

Caroline 'Ceri Naz' Nazareno Gabis

Carolin 'Ceri' Nazareno-Gabis

Caroline 'Ceri Naz' Nazareno-Gabis, author of Velvet Passions of Calibrated Quarks, World Poetry Canada International Director to Philippines is known as a 'poet of peace and friendship', a multi-awarded poet, editor, journalist, speaker, linguist, educator, peace and women's advocate. She believes that learning other's language and culture is a doorway to wisdom.

Among her poetic belts include PANORAMA YOUTH LITERARY AWARDS 2020, 7 th Prize Winner in the 19th, 20th and 21st Italian Award of Literary Festival; Writers International Network-Canada ''Amazing Poet 2015'', The Frang Bardhi Literary Prize 2014 (Albania), the sair-gazeteci or Poet Journalist Award 2014 (Tuzla, Istanbul, Turkey) and World Poetry Empowered Poet 2013 (Vancouver, Canada). She's a featured member of Association of Women's Rights and Development (AWID), The Poetry Posse, Galaktika Poetike, Asia Pacific Writers and Translators (APWT), Axlepino and Anacbanua.

Her poetry and children's stories have been featured in different anthologies and magazines worldwide.

Links to her works:

panitikan.ph/2018/03/30/caroline-nazareno-gabis

apwriters.org/author/ceri_naz/

www.aveviajera.org/nacionesunidasdelasletras/id1181.html

The Bard and The Milady
(Part 1)

The bard once penned
"poetry, wine and chants"
for his voluptuous muse
as gorgeous as Marilyn Monroe,
 reminiscing his amaranthine lines
the milady interrupts:
Indulge and set back…
"Syrah, bold and rich red
Zinfandel, aged indigenous oak
Malbec, full-bodied, deep red
Merlot, find some exotic ducks to pair,
Sauvignon Blanc, light, dry and crisp white wine,"
My love, which does your heart delights for?"
Finally answered, "Give me some light and lines"
The milady, in velvet red,
Kissed her, a poem sublime.

In her eyes

In the morning, she wakes up
Hiding her shadow like gilded little sun
Then poke her parents' eyes.
She lifts those tiny legs
To kick the hanging dreamcatcher,
 Reflects a silly face
In the mirror towards the bedroom wall.
Ta-ta-ta, counting bananas while watching
The musical Barney,
Her smiles paint fire,
Her yells bear wind,
Her shallow tears sail innocence
In the river of my soul.

spring's secret lullaby

waiting for the pearly morn
cascading with infinite dew drops
crystalline symphonies on the clouds
whispering silver charming flames
a song bird singing merry silhouettes
in the majestic hours of spring
with you by my side is a dream
like secrets lulling mellow chants
while dancing to life's windmills of chance

Swapna Behera

Swapna Behera

Swapna Behera is a bilingual contemporary poet, author, translator and editor from Odisha, India. She was a teacher from 1984 to 2015. Her stories, poems and articles are widely published in National and International journals, and ezines, and are translated into different national and International languages. She has penned six books. She is the recipient of the Prestigious International Mother Language UGADI AWARD WINNER 2019. She was conferred upon the Prestigious International Poesis Award of Honor at the 2nd Bharat Award for Literature as Jury in 2015, The Enchanting Muse Award in India World Poetree Festival 2017, World Icon of Peace Award in 2017, and the Pentasi B World Fellow Poet in 2017. She is the recipient of the Prolific Poetess Award ,The Life time Achievement Award ,The Best Planner Award ,The Sahitya Shiromani Award, ATAL BIHARI BAJPAYEE Award, ATAL Award 2018 ,Global Literature Guardian Award ,International Life Time Achievement Award and the Master of Creative Impulse Award .She has received the Honoured Poet of India from the Seychelles Government accredited Literary Society Lasher one poem A NIGHT IN THE REFUGEE CAMP is translated into 60 languages .She is the Ambassador of Humanity by Hafrikan Prince Art World Africa 2018 and an official member of World Nation's Writers Union ,Kazakhstan2018. Italy, the National President for India by Hispanomundial Union of Writers (UHE), Peru, the administrator of several poetic groups, and the Cultural Ambassador for India and South Asia of Inner Child Press African is the life member of Odisha Environmental Society.

swapna.behera@gmail.com

each dot is a foot print

each dot dances
each dot speaks
each dot is a figure
our ancestor's
footsteps are dots
look up
the sky and stars
shower justice to our land
each rain drop is their blessing

each dot sings
each dot dreams
each dot is a Sun
each dot is life
that reflects existence

just join the dots
to make   a wing
 shine in the horizon
 speak your existence
each dot is the replica of time

only a single dot.......
from heaven .....

disaster in the courtyard

there is a disaster
a caterpillar crawling
the lizard on the bloody cot
tea cups scattered on the ground
no conversation
none is chewing sugarcane
no fire in the cooking place
the pet dog is dying there
certainly, a disaster last night
a broken lantern, a torn door screen
split of bangles, couple of holes of the bullets on the door
the cows are scared, no fodder in their monger
who is the intruder?
the terrorists, the rapist or the drug mafias
the small girl peeping
stunned
the only eye witness to record the bloody history
everything is dark
the courtyard that conducts rituals from birth to death
marriage to sickness
no aroma of tandoori roti and dal makhana
a stoic silence
a frog croaking outside
a house gives shelter to many
journey of money or honey
seniors or kids; a sweet family
the nucleus of existence
basks inner light
yes, the last rituals of vermilion or turmeric
jasmines fragrances
courtyard reflects seasons in multiple colours

so also, when the martyr's body
covered with tricolour flags
alas! there is a disaster is in this courtyard ......

N.B;- Tandoori Roti and Dal Makhani are the popular cuisines.

just now what I remember

the lush pasture green grass
swings of aerial roots
of the banyan tree in my village
that is my mother Nature

have you seen ants in lines
carrying sugar cubes or rice grains
heavier than their weight
bigger than their size

just now what I remember
 is my father's walking stick
that stands as a full stop to every vice.

intoxicated right side road of my age
archetypal tantrums
call it a sky ,an ocean
or any name
it is the synonym of confidence

just now what I remember
 it's crescent moon smile

Swapna Behera

Albert 'Infinite' Carrasco

Albert 'Infinite' Carassco

Albert "Infinite The Poet" Carrasco is an urban poet, mentor and public speaker.

Albert believes his experience of growing up in poverty, dealing with drugs and witnessing murder over and over were lessons learnt, in order to gain knowledge to teach. Albert's harsh reality and honesty is a powerfully packed punch delivered through rhyme. Infinite grew up in the east part of the Bronx and still resides there, so he knows many young men will follow the same dark path he followed looking for change. The life of crime should never be an option to being poor but it is, very often.

Infinite poetry @lulu.com

Alcarrasco2 on YouTube

Infinite the poet on reverbnation

Infinite Poetry

http://www.lulu.com/us/en/shop/al-infinite-carrasco/infinite-poetry/paperback/product-21040240.html

Mundara Koorang

Mundara is an Australian Aboriginal artist, designer, teacher, actor and author from Eora.

He used all of his talents as an educator since he is an indigenous elder.

Mundara Koorang wanted successful education for his people so they can be all they wanted to be,

not just because they should, but because he believed that was their destiny.

he alone was responsible for over 800 people attending schools and universities

Literature and art both were used so he can paint visual and mental pictures.

He is well known, not just in his community but internationally.

He is a leader,

his work paved the way for the future,

His practices opened the doors for other indigenous artist in Australia.

Why

Why did he do it
From where I am, I can rewind time and see his every action
I'm studying him to understand why
He wakes up in the morning, kisses his wife and three baby's, just as I did
I'm watching him get dressed for work just as i am
It's crazy how two unfamiliar faces are doing the same thing I Different places
I put on my work clothes
He puts on his ensemble
I walk downstairs to check my mail box
He carefully walks downstairs, holding his waistline, making sure what he's holding don't drop
My car is parked two blocks away, it's at a spot on the corner, so I'm walking
There he goes walking my direction stalking
I can sense the danger
Today we will no longer be strangers
I ruffle through my pockets for the keys
My window shatters
What he had in his waistline is now pointed at me
I'm watching myself plead
I'm begging him not to shoot
He's persistently screaming give me the loot
I give it to him, but he still shoots to kill
He runs off with what I just got out the mailbox,
Which was payroll for my guys
He runs back upstairs, with the look of greed in his eyes
His wife looks and ask what's wrong
He says I just killed to pay our bills
Turns out he was recently fired from his nine to five
So now I know but still don't understand

Why "I" had to die

Albert 'Infinite' Carassco

I u u used to st stu stutter

Some used to laugh at me, hahahah he stutters like Stanley. I wanted to curse them out. but it would've took too long so I bowed my head and walked on in embarrassment, I became really shy, i didn't want any peer acknowledgment, I was scared to speak then deal with the harassment. When in class and the teacher would ask the students a question, in a split second I would know the answer, but i would sit quietly and let my classmates figure it out until one of them minutes later would scream out the wrong answer, usually. When that happened I would pray please please don't let her call on me, But she did. Carrasco can you help us out? N no I I don't know. Damm because I stutter I can't get due credit for knowing that answer. This was my life. Moooom what yo yo you cccoking today? Boy slow down, think before you say what you want to say, take your time!. Moms therapy helped me. i started speaking clearly slowly. My mouth caught up with my brain now I talk like I'm in a speed lane, some people said I talk to fast, now I laughed inside, didn't want to be rude like they was to me, all they saw was me smiling while their brain was stu stu stuttering

Eliza Segiet

Eliza Segiet: Master's Degree in Philosophy, completed postgraduate studies in Cultural Knowledge, Philosophy, Arts and Literature at Jagiellonian University. She is a member of The Association of Polish Writers and The NWNU - Union of Writers of the World.

Her poems *Questions* and *Sea of Mists* won the title of the International Publication of the Year 2017 and 2018 in Spillwords Press.

For her volume of *Magnetic People* she won a literary award of a *Golden Rose* named after Jaroslaw Zielinski (Poland 2019 r.). Her poem The *Sea of Mists* was chosen as one of the best one hundred poems of 2018 by International Poetry Press Publication Canada.
In Poet's Yearbook, as the author of *Sea of Mists*, she was awarded with the prestigious Elite Writer's Status Award as one of the best poets of 2019 (July 2019).
She was awarded *World Poetic Star Award* by World Nations Writers Union – the world's largest Writers' Union from Kazakhstan (August 2019).
In September 2019 she was 1st Place Laureate (Foreign Poetry category) – in Contest *Quando È la Vita ad Invitare* for poem *Be Yourself* (Italy).
Her poem *Order* from volume *Unpaired* was selected as one of the 100 best poems of 2019 in International Poetry Press Publications (Canada).
Nominated for the Pushcart Prize 2019.
Nominated for the iWoman Global Awards (2019).
Laureate Naji Naaman Literary Prize 2020.
Laureate International Award PARAGON OF HOPE (Canada, 2020).
Obtained certificate of appreciation from *Gujarat Sahitya Academy* and *Motivational Strips* for literary excellence par with global standards (2020).
Ambassador of Literature granted by *Motivational Strips*.
Author's works can be found in anthologies, separate books and literary magazines worldwide.

Parallel time
To Mundara Koorangow

With greatness
of multicolored dots
not from alphabet Braille, Morse,
but from aboriginal tradition
the painted world
of ancient beliefs awes.
Ancestral past
united with today's day
tells a reality.

Parallel time
– magic between,
what was and what is found.

Dreamtime
doesn't permit forgetting.

No matter where you will start in your time.
What counts is where you'll make it
and what you'll hide in memory,
to be able to pass on to others.

Translated Ula de B.

Deceit

Preoccupied with invoices
he didn't hear the deceit.
Certain,
he can sense who tells the truth,
and who's closer to falsehood.
He didn't pay attention to the signs.
Believing in nonexistence of evil,
he trusted
his gift of situational assessment.

When he has awoken,
he became
a homeless ex millionaire,
with no chance to return to
his familiar,
but already lost life.

He whispered to himself:
– Don't trust anyone,
who's overmuch benevolent.
He merely pretends,

to gain,
till you have.

Translated Ula de B.

Crease

Is there any sense?
Maybe just for a try?

Resurrecting friendship
is like
filling a blown egg.
There will always be
a gap, void,
that
will not allow you to return
to the state it was before.

An attempt
may seemingly succeed,
but
the painful crease inside
will someday resurrect.

Translated by Artur Komoter

William S. Peters Sr.

William S. Peters, Sr.

Bill's writing career spans a period of over 50 years. Being first Published in 1972, Bill has since went on to Author in excess of 50 additional Volumes of Poetry, Short Stories, etc., expressing his thoughts on matters of the Heart, Spirit, Consciousness and Humanity. His primary focus is that of Love, Peace and Understanding!

Bill says . . .

I have always likened Life to that of a Garden. So, for me, Life is simply about the Seeds we Sow and Nourish. All things we "Think and Do", will "Be" Cause and eventually manifest itself to being an "Effect" within our own personal "Existences" and "Experiences" . . . whether it be Fruit, Flowers, Weeds or Barren Landscapes! Bill highly regards the Fruits of his Labor and wishes that everyone would thus go on to plant "Lovely" Seeds on "Good Ground" in their own Gardens of Life!

to connect with Bill, he is all things Inner Child

www.iaminnerchild.com

Personal Web Site

www.iamjustbill.com

An Artist's Breath

Write stories upon the canvass
I paint pictures with my written word
And my mind is still thirsty,
Hungry,
To continue its quest
Into the unknown

What I gain, I gift
What I learn, I teach
I have two hands
That I may lift you up,
For this is the art
Of living
This is
"An Artist's Breath" . . .
Breathe with me

paint my dreams

i took my dreams
and painted them
with the colors
of expectations
for i wanted to
meet them
greet them
and
seat them
at the table of my realities

yes

i want to
eat with them
drink with them
discuss the day with them
and speak of
our love
and the certainty
of the absence
of the hurt in me
and the joys
of our coming days

a place
where our chase
of each other
has ceased
for we are in phase
as one
and in peace

and after we finish dining
we begin refining

William S. Peters, Sr.

our relationship
i want to put some music on
you know
that Cosmic type
and i want to dance with my Dreams
my Lover of me
i wish to swirl
and be whirled around
as i embrace the sound
of the moment

i wish to do a two step or three
or more
as i have removed the door
that once inhibited who i am
i want to dance the dance of joy
unrestrained
never to be contained
again

and we will glisten
as we listen
to the our bonded heart
that of every Girl and Boy
and the gifts
we were born with
impervious of the shift
we allowed to induce us
seduce us
by way of our trusts
we freely gave to the world

and as the "i" in me
heralds in this new thought
a perspective of life
i have long ago forgotten
i realize

with open eyes
that i am the artist
i am the creator
i am the progenitor
of what i think i am

and there is no God
but i am He who has made me
for it was His or Her
or whatever you prefer
it was the Sources Holy breath
that give's me Life
and with a rife of attitude
and a heart of gratitude
i celebrate this day
in my way

and know this
that it is i who created this palette
upon which i mix the colors
that i may paint the canvass of my existence
as i choose

so excuse me
for i refuse
to accuse
circumstance
things
and people
to inhibit
my exhibit
of my Self Art
and how i elect
to paint my dreams

It is time

Down by the river
Where the sleeping waters lie
Where figments of humanity's imagination
Dance in the dust,
Teasing one and all
With ghost-like etheric visions of
Justice,
Equality,
Compassion,
Righteousness
And unrequited,
Unabashed,
Unrestrained,
Uninhibited,
Unafraid . . .
Love

I visit this place
Every day,
With my longing tucked neatly
In the hidden
Semi-transparent chambers
Of my heart

My breast expands with hope
And exasperation
Conjuring new convoluted devils
For my consideration ...
Whom shall I follow?

As I hold to the reins tightly
So that hate will abate itself

And self-declare its hypocrisy,
I smile in the faces
Of the virtue-less,
For I know
They are haunted
By their own shadows

I strive for the struggle,
Sweating away heavy burdensome concerns,
For they 'do' nor service naught

Should a rainbow visit my space,
I would probably cloak it
In gossamer and lace
And put small trinket-like bells
On the threads of its presence
That I will be alerted
Should my private rainbows
Attempt to escape
Into the dark of the night

I am counting the birds
Perched in the trees
Chattering and chirping
About what, who knows?
.....
Much like man,
For reconciliation and resolution
For our on-going concerns
Again escape our attempts
To jail them
In our ever moving present

'Now' continues to elude me
While continuously and profusely

Licking my brow
Telling me the dripping essence
Upon my face
Is a worthy sweat
For which I toiled
.....
But me thinks
It is my tears
Of my ever-flowing lament
And melancholy

Perhaps if I let enough of them pool
Just perhaps
We can awaken
Those sleeping waters
Down by the river
Where figments of humanity's imagination
Dance in the dust,
Teasing one and all
With ghost-like etheric visions of
Justice,
Equality,
Compassion,
Righteousness
And unrequited,
Unabashed,
Unrestrained,
Uninhibited,
Unafraid . . .
Love

It is time

August 2021 Featured Poets

~ * ~

Caroline Laurent Turunc

Kamal Dhungana

Pankhuri Sinha

Paramita Mukherjee Mullick

Caroline Laurent Turunc

Caroline Laurent Turunc

Caroline LAURENT Turunc Antakya, Turkey, Arab origin, the daughter of a family of nine children. She started writing at the age of 15. She wrote her first novel at this age and her family did not allow the book to be published, her brother and mother destroyed the manuscript.

This incident did not prevent her from writing more. She has written over 1500 poems since 2013, received many certificates from abroad, and participated in 12 local and foreign anthologies. Her poems have been published in many international journals and sites.
She is writing a novel and is about to finish it soon. She published two poetry books, "Between Oriental and Schemal" and "Desert lily".

She won the second place among 2575 poets from every country during the championship of the world literature in Romania.

She won a prize in the poetry festival held by Yan in China which led her to be selected into the "world poet Literature Museum" built by the Silk Road Cultural Center of Northwest University of China.

She was also a jury member of the Galaxia International Award for unpublished Poetry, 2021 edition in Chile

She is a Turkey-based Humanitarian and represents the u.t.e.f. International foundation in Paris
She currently lives in Paris, France

carolineturunc@yahoo.com

A Refugee's Diary!

It was a breathless morning, a young man with his hands inside his pockets as if he is cold.
He was looking for a dry place in the streets of a language he did not know.
The hand lines on his palm were erased, his fingers were turned purple.
Even stones with a shadow of the sun on them were luckier than him.
It was as if the sky was blurred, being held by a thread from his entire past.
there was no trace of his habits

He was staring at strange faces like a ship lost at the dock.
It was as if he was looking for the future with hope in the raging polluted sea.
He was a refugee looking for his lost past
It came from photographs that had been erased from timeless calendars by the violence of a hurricane.

Nameless leaves plucked from the branch
Unconscious flying migratory birds disappearing during the day
Like a sycamore tree captive to the shadow's reflection
Dwarves trapped inside the mirror
among bloodthirsty demons

Who knows why he came to the place where the eternal sun turns yellow?
Just like my father's face, his face is grounded

A shiver got me!

Death came to my mind.
what were their sins - what were their sins so much that they were dragged from the land of their birth?
Were the streets crooked or were the lamps without light?

In the scorching summer sun, my heart turned cold like winter.
the wind was blowing me
I looked at his face, his smile, his eyes were dark.
I raised my hand and said "hey, I know how you feel, I've been down these roads too, I've been a refugee in soul more than in my body".

While I was eating at those crowded tables, it suddenly came to my mind and I went to the days when we were not satisfied with what was on our plate.
How the time passed, I was startled by a voice, the police asked me to show my ID, so I put my hand insidemy bag, grabbed my ID and showed it to them. My eyes filled with tears when I remembered of the things I went through to have this card.

I left all my loved ones without looking back, it was so heavy that I missed asking my mother whether she loves me more than my brother.
I miss the days when my mother could not bear to beat me and cry, those days come back and my mother beat me again

I'm crying now I have no one to cry with me
I looked around again, my eyes searched for that young man, it had never rained so differently in the rains.
It smells of a wind that I've never known before
As if at a turning point

Caroline Laurent Turunc

Or was it a dream, in the middle of my brain
Was it the game of unstable seasons caused by poverty?
Living in a twelve square meter room from the big house of a large family
The room has no ceiling, the walls are pale, if a light breeze blows the door will fly.

Yes, I was a refugee; each of us comes from a land of sorrow.
We fell into poverty. Strangers to each other.
If I were a god for a day, I would plant the seed of immortality.
From moldy vases to flower pots, to every garden of every house
May the earth not miss that crazy smell of death

O supreme soul that makes my body tremble with every breath I take"
Farewells should not be premature, those strange flowers should not adorn the tops of the chests.
Crying children.
The streets waiting for refugees

Caroline Laurent Turunc
13/06/2021 PARIS

Don't Kill Silent Languages !

When I walk away from my sadness
    Minions, horses, crawls, caresses, hits
    Even if my heart is choking I find a way to get it
    But you're drowning.
    How many mornings did I wake up
    I'm listening to the confusion
    Nobody knocks on my door Why am I someone who loves cats
    I know i am
    I'm not satisfied without cat and love
    At the deciduous end of my days without such resistance on our most complicated path
    If I don't resist the rain and the cloud is quiet the night before the morning preparations, if you don't resist
    Denying three lonely cats above the clouds without knowing their names
    Strolling on orchids
    When they have the right to fly like a sparrow while breathing like you and me
    Nobody is sweeter than this bird
    Blue and bluebird in paradise
    That ties a bead to each feather
    The roofs were orphans, the streets were like stepchildren without cats, now I'm like a stupid gazelle lover Ahu, without the eyes of chimpanzees jumping from branch to branch.
    Count me as a lonely necked cat, somehow I have a mouth and no tongue. This was not a story.
    I said did you listen to me, nobody looked at me
    Should he hide or say; everything is empty
    There was neither that house, nor that day, nor the cat. Except for muddy rivers

Caroline Laurent Turunc

I look like a shore in the shade of red tiles
on the scattered roofs of his village. And in the spring chaos of rain clouds
Birds were placed on the shore of a passing lake, no one left anymore, the silence swallowed all their joyful voices
Caroline Laurent Turunç
PARİS

Bloody Virus!

In my heart I have all the documents of your eyes
Will not rot with wet, fragrant violets
Some daffodils from neighboring mountains
A little star falling from the sky
To melt a cloud of snow into my heart
Far from the sun, the moon, the fire
I'm so tired with the shroud on me

the curvature of the light was the sun
I don't know if my defeat is now a victory
Who is this sky and why is it unattended?
I apologize to the world in my conscience
How stubborn is the smoke from yellowed horizons
Humanity was not so arrogant when the pharaoh descended
on the ground of persecution
your brightness, darkness, splendor lover

The vampire that makes the bloody fuck shiver
How sweet you are with your two purple eyes
Beyond the red sea
The mass that walks like a dead
Cover the earth, cover the particles of hypocrisy
Their filth is rippling, those who don't care about the overflowing laments
Cover up all calamities, their stomachs low, poisonous

They ate from open tables without chewing
Seven colors in one sitting
Come brother come blessed
Running, resisting, saving is our passion
He's got balls of cruelty, he's got bayonets, his eyes are stabbing

Caroline Laurent Turunc

Country shattered for a bloody crown
Cut the chains connecting the hand and arm
Get away from the strong and the bad

Carnations planted in destruction look miserable in pain and anguish
Street of dreams is not real
Fill old warehouses and rundown cellars to be repaired
Traitors roll for wine, laugh, cry for hypocrites
Let the migration from the earth to the sky begin
None of them have a profession, no virtue, no legitimacy
No different from a prostitute

Kamal Dhungana

Kamal Dhungana

Kamal Dhungana was born in India in 1994, but he is a citizen of Nepal, Kamal has studied up to Inter second year

Kamal says he has been writing poems for 5 to 6 years now. Apart from poetry, he also writes ghazals and short stories. Some of my poems have been published from Vietnam, Bangladesh, China, Serbia, Spain, India, Egypt, Roman, Palestine, Indonesia and Nepal.

After some time now, I am bringing a collection of poems to the market.

Kamal Dhungana
Tikapur Kailali Nepal
Email: kamaldhungana860@gmail.com

Kamal Dhungana

People are not the same

Cover people to be the same
Not just together
Do people have to agree to be the same?
The idea has to be agreed.
Nobody agrees with anyone here
Here one does not count the other as human
People don't even have human blood
That is why people are not the same.

When the flood of last year washed away my house
My neighbors took me to my house one day
No one told me to stay
Even after hearing the news that I am homeless, my relatives
They never came to see me
That's why I've never been around them
Maybe I wasn't like them
Maybe we weren't the same creature ....

If people were the same
Why did people get beaten up for touching water?
Why women sold in the room
Did you have to live like an animal?
Why did people enslave people?
People are not really the same
People don't even get people's blood
If found, my pregnant mother
You didn't have to die at a young age without getting O positive blood.

Hunger

I know the government
I am illiterate, I am uneducated
My father told me to teach
He must have been living in the house of the chief.
My mother told me to teach at the chief's house
She must have wiped the broom.
He must have fed me even though he was hungry
I cried and cried when I was hungry
But, my parents are hungry
Crying in front, screaming?
Government to tell who is hungry?

Because of the huge mountain of poverty
I couldn't read, even though I wanted to
There were no opportunities to study on scholarships
The fire in the hungry stomach has never been extinguished
My father was drenched in sweat all day long
When I return home tired in the evening
My eyes weep late into the night
I don't sleep all night when my mother is hungry.
I know - I was burning with hunger
My father and mother, who look twice as good as me
The fire that burns in the hungry stomach every day
I have seen - innumerable mothers like my mother
She is sucking her breasts on her hungry stomach in the street
I have seen - lust for a loaf of bread
Hungry faces doing ..

How long will the government be cheap?
Sweat dripping, wages?

Kamal Dhungana

How long will the wages be?
How long will you continue to shed blood and sweat in foreign lands?
Weaving thousands of dreams to come for how long
Foreigners in the red box?
How long will the stitches of millions of women be asked?
How long will the society not get mourners?
How long will the government school be built in my village?
How long can you get employment in the country by studying?
How long do you have to sleep hungry?
And when the government is reduced to hunger
Number of suicides?

Then the doorbell rang

I found out then
The thing about not coming back after you're gone
How many nights when I look at your way
After I slept soundly

I don't sleep
Pillow never shed tears
Wet was not wet
I sleep every night after you leave
Pillow who never got wet in bed
They started getting wet every night

I did not know
Most of all, looking for someone's way
It is a difficult task, even a day seems like a year

I found out after you left
What is emptiness?
Nowadays, my bedroom is no less than a secluded forest
Life I live, life does not seem

It's been a long time since the doorbell rang at home
Not a few fingers ringing the doorbell
There are strong eyes watching your path
There is a life waiting for you
And there are loud ears, hoping for the doorbell to ring

Kamal Dhungana

Pankhuri Sinha

Pankhuri Sinha

Pankhuri Sinha is a bilingual poet and story writer from India, who has lived in North America for 14 years and has two books of poems published in English, two collections of stories published in Hindi, five collections of poetries published in Hindi, with many more lined up. Has won many prestigious, national-international awards, has been translated in over twenty two languages. Her writing is dominated by themes of exile and immigration, gender equality and environmental concerns.

Wander

Walk again
Wander
In the alleys of other people's home
For it is another gorgeous fall day
The colors
They change each day
Deepen, darken
Leaves crunch under your feet
Leaves fall around you
Trees bare themselves
Brace for winter
An year is about to pass
Walk again
In the alleys of other people's home
Or just sit and type
Sit here, yes, right here
Type
Imprint
Document
Tell us, they say
Of their torture
Send us evidence
Send them
The story of what's happening
But whats happening
You type and type
Get nowhere
The tv
Right infront
Shows all about tracking
Tracking through phone calls
Devices

Police gadgets
Apparatus
But sit and type
Of how the surveillance around you works
Type with untrimmed nails
Type before trimming them
Cutting your nails
Little things, no colors
No polish
No rings
No promises
Vacant empty fingers
With the metaphor of nail trimming
Cutting, having become very large
In the language of espionage
Some said, some felt
Nails of people
Digging occasionally in your flesh
Your own being pulled out
Are they?
Or anytime now?
All gone?
Fall leaves
Yet another fall day
Wander
Or type some more
Just taking notes
Recording
Data collection almost
Of perpetrated torture
Inflicted
Imposed
Inescapable
Permeating
Suffocating

Pankhuri Sinha

Torture
Or walk again
In the alleys of other people's homes
For you lost your own
But you live here too
Renting a flat or a room
Who makes it then
A purpose out of fighting landlordism?

That poem

That poem
Will have to be written elsewhere
And on another day
Although she very much wanted to write it
In that lounge
Of that restaurant
It was an all day buffet
Actually
And spoke to her current hunger
Very loudly
Spoke of her current status
Of an emaciated
Devastated
Immigration warrior
A status
She had described
Narrated
To the lady
Posing
As the landlady
Very aptly
As precisely
As there were words
Around and available
And was heartbroken again
As the lady
Subletting the apartment
Had so calmly
Picked up
All of these brochures
And coupons
Of restaurants

Pankhuri Sinha

And all other food chains
Dear Suzannah 21
With pictures of what was called
Fast food
Not even crawling towards her
All opportunities
Coming so slow
She feared
She will die before redemption
Will never be able to walk
To that counter
That will say
You have been hired
Will say it
In valid paperwork
While the lady
Spreading the coupons
On all purchases
Talked of how the buffet
Was quite average
Not too great
But alright
And she found herself
Lapsing into that silence
Which forbade all responses
Not being able to leave
That zone of lonely silence
Not being able to reach out
And across
Fenced in
Barricaded
And building more
To never break out of
To never breakthrough

The Year of the Poet VIII ~ August 2021

But the current stalemate
Had simply to do
With some sort of a negotiation
Not even negotiation
No great big deals
Simple talk over chore sharing
Little dusting
Little collected dust
Gigantic grievances
Over specks of dust
Not being addressed
Left to accumulate
With a viewpoint
Dogmatic
Heavy handed
With a viewpoint
That took all its angles
From the top
And believed in cutting off
The supply lines
Believed in pulling the rug
From under someone's feet
Believed in making them fall
Falter
Spoke bad army language
And for sure
Got its re-enforcements
From many powerful places
Offices
Of culture and learning.

At home

Stuck
At home
Again
Shifting between salt and sugar
Resisting one more bite of chocolate
When sweet seems salvation
All thoughts centered around coco powder
And the means to acquire it
With the hopes of making someday
Home made chocolates
A nice point to be in
A nice cave to be in
Not comprehending the violence around
Not comprehending violence at all
Mixed often, with news from the drug world
With talk about the drug world
Those who ran
And those who perished in it
Those who stood at its frontier
Unclear talk about the drug world
Also carried out over people's medications
Prescriptions
Around the sales in the over the counter pills aisles
Sometimes a very silent kind of store violence
Visible but not audible
And then just plain, simple violence
In and out of the store
On the benches in the smoking area
On the benches in the parks
And in the parks with no benches
And all of this airy, breezy conflict
Conditional to weather

The Year of the Poet VIII ~ August 2021

A life totally weather dependent
Put under house arrest
Made to move
Just so many times
Impossible to keep track of all my papers
The one with chocolate recipes
Poems of chocolate cravings
Important papers
Not just ids
But maps of writings
To be expanded upon
All packed in suitcases
And so unsettled
Impossible to elaborate upon
Impossible to bring to life
Clicking pictures of coco beans
In a mall
Being the liveliest sheet of paper
The shiniest
To look and look again
Stuck at home
Trapped in a war over coco
With all sense of speed
Even movement
Left outside
In the great outdoors.

Pankhuri Sinha

Paramita Mukherjee Mullick

Paramita Mukherjee Mullick

Dr. Paramita Mukherjee Mullick is a scientist transformed into a poet. She has six published books. She is the Founder President of the Intercultural Poetry and Performance Library Mumbai Chapter where she promotes fusion of poetry with other performing arts. Her poems have been translated into 39 languages. Paramita has been blessed with numerous awards for her poetry which are as follows:

Sahitya Shree
Sahityan Samman
Sahitya Bhushan
Master of Creative Genius
Nobel Laurate Rabindranath Tagore Award,
Poetess of Elegance 2019
Literoma Author Achiever 2020
SLF Excellence Award

In the World Congress of 2019, she received the Gold Rose from MS Productions, Buenos Aires for promotion of literature and culture. She does a lot of peace poetry events and received a recognition from the World Literary Forum of Writers and Human rights. Paramita believes in positivity and finds silver linings in every cloud of gloom. She lives in Mumbai, India with her husband and daughter.

The Search For Completeness

The new mother looks at the smile of her child.
Her heart fills with joy.
The new human fills her heart.
A happiness more than any jazzy toy.

A mother and wife, looks after her family.
Feeds them and lovingly them nourish.
Selfless, compassionate and kind.
Her happiness to see her children and husband flourish.

A father and a husband, toils the whole day.
To make the family prosperous and comfortable.
Only others in his mind when working hard.
Bringing his family members in the forefront and making them able.

The giving of oneself to another.
An emotion which is all above.
The search for completeness ends with this emotion.
It is the definition less, fathomless love.

Impermanence

The yellow leaves on the branch became yellow and fell off.
Green new leaves sprouted on the branch again.
A brief shower of rain quenched the thirst of the earth.
The sweet-smelling earth heaved a sigh of relief.
The kingfisher fleeted by, here it was and then lost from sight.
Its dazzling colours lingering in my eyes.
Suddenly the melodious music from the flute player on the street.
Arouses my senses and I get immersed in that music.
Such is the magic of impermanence.
The short spell enchants us.
A brief encounter with a stranger,
May lead to a beautiful friendship.
These moments are to be cherished and preserved.
Time for such beautiful moments to be reserved.

Paramita Mukherjee Mullick

When I Will Meet You

When I will meet you one day.

You will look into my eyes and what will you say?

Will you welcome me with open arms?

Remembering

our fallen soldiers of verse

Janet Perkins Caldwell
February 14, 1959 ~ September 20, 2016

Alan W. Jankowski
16 March 1961 ~ 10 March 2017

Now available

World Healing World Peace
2020

Poets for Humanity

Inner Child Press News

Poetry Posse Members

We are so excited to share and announce a few of the current books, as well as the new and upcoming books of some of our Poetry Posse authors.

On the following pages we present to you ...

Jackie Davis Allen

Gail Weston Shazor

hülya n. yılmaz

Nizar Sartawi

Faleeha Hassan

Fahredin Shehu

Caroline 'Ceri' Nazareno

Eliza Segiet

Teresa E. Gallion

William S. Peters, Sr.

The Year of the Poet VIII ~ August 2021

Now Available
www.innerchildpress.com

Inner Child Press News

Now Available
www.innerchildpress.com

The Year of the Poet VIII ~ August 2021

Now Available
www.innerchildpress.com

Inner Child Press News

Now Available at

www.amazon.com/gp/product/B08MYL5B7S/ref=dbs_a_def_rwt_hsch_vapi_tkin_p1_i2

The Year of the Poet VIII ~ August 2021

Now Available at
www.innerchildpress.com

Inner Child Press News

Now Available
www.innerchildpress.com

The Year of the Poet VIII ~ August 2021

Now Available
www.innerchildpress.com

Inner Child Press News

Now Available
www.innerchildpress.com

The Year of the Poet VIII ~ August 2021

COMING SOON
www.innerchildpress.com

The Book of krisar
volume v

william s. peters, sr.

Inner Child Press News

Now Available
www.innerchildpress.com

The Book of krisar

Volume I

william s. peters, sr.

The Book of krisar

Volume II

william s. peters, sr.

The Year of the Poet VIII ~ August 2021

Now Available
www.innerchildpress.com

The Book of krisar

Volume III

william s. peters, sr.

The Book of krisar

Volume IV

william s. peters, sr.

Inner Child Press News

Now Available
www.innerchildpress.com

Velvet Passions of Calibrated Quarks

Caroline Nazareno-Gabis

The Year of the Poet VIII ~ August 2021

Now Available
www.innerchildpress.com

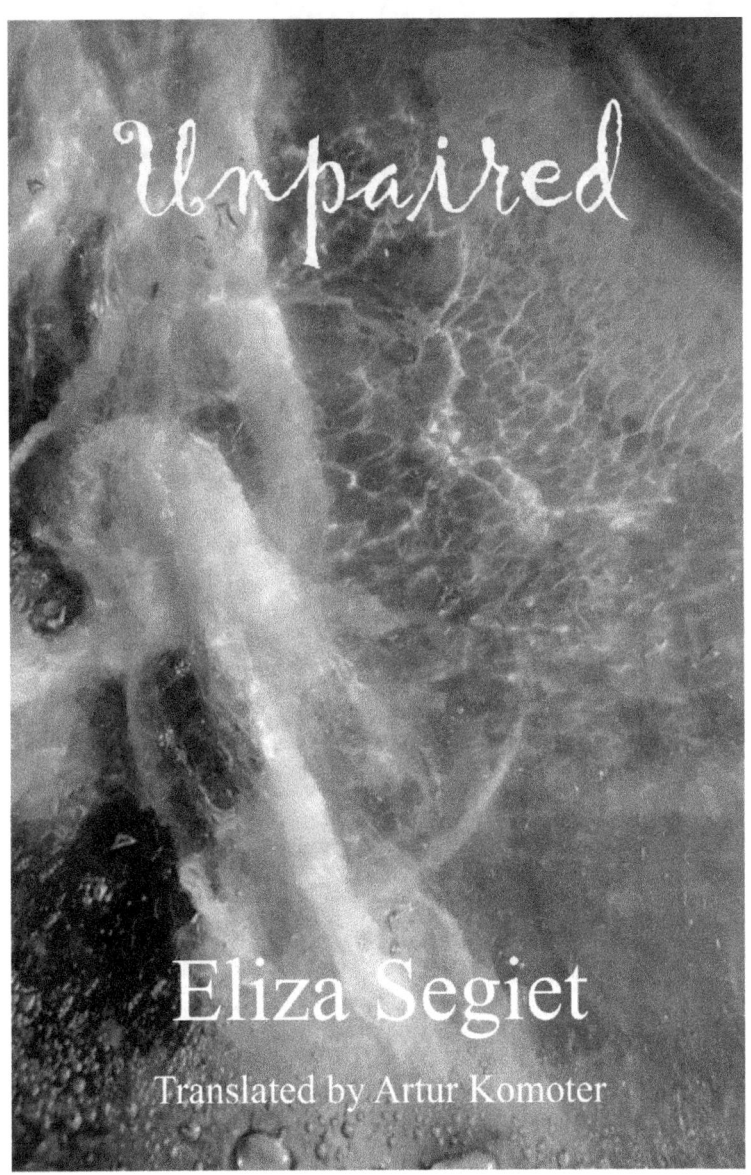

Inner Child Press News

Private Issue
www.innerchildpress.com

Canlarım
My Lifeblood
poetry in Turkish and English

hülya n. yılmaz

The Year of the Poet VIII ~ August 2021

Now Available
www.innerchildpress.com

Inner Child Press News

Now Available at
www.innerchildpress.com

No Illusions
Through the Looking Glass

Jackie Davis Allen

The Year of the Poet VIII ~ August 2021

Now Available at
www.innerchildpress.com

Inner Child Press News

Now Available at
www.innerchildpress.com

Eclectic Verse
mommy i hear those whispers . . . (again)
WilliAM s. Peters, sR

The Year of the Poet VIII ~ August 2021

Now Available at
www.innerchildpress.com

HERENOW

FAHREDIN SHEHU

Inner Child Press News

Now Available at
www.innerchildpress.com

The Year of the Poet VIII ~ August 2021

Now Available at
www.innerchildpress.com

Inner Child Press News

Now Available at
www.innerchildpress.com

The Year of the Poet VIII ~ August 2021

Now Available at
www.innerchildpress.com

Inner Child Press News

Now Available at
www.innerchildpress.com

The Year of the Poet VIII ~ August 2021

Now Available at
www.innerchildpress.com

Breakfast
for
Butterflies

Faleeha Hassan

Inner Child Press News

Now Available at
www.innerchildpress.com

The Year of the Poet VIII ~ August 2021

Now Available at
www.innerchildpress.com

inner child press
presents

Tunisia My Love

william s. peters, sr.

Inner Child Press News

Now Available at
www.innerchildpress.com

The Year of the Poet VIII ~ August 2021

Now Available at
www.innerchildpress.com

Think on These Things
Book II

william s. peters, sr.

Other

Anthological

works from

Inner Child Press International

www.innerchildpress.com

Inner Child Press Anthologies

World Healing World Peace 2020

Poets for Humanity

Now Available
www.worldhealingworldpeacepoetry.com

Inner Child Press Anthologies

Now Available
www.innerchildpress.com

Inner Child Press Anthologies

Inner Child Press International
&
The Year of the Poet
present

Poetry
the best of 2020

Poets of the World

Now Available
www.innerchildpress.com

Inner Child Press Anthologies

Now Available
www.innerchildpress.com

Inner Child Press Anthologies

the Heart of a Poet

words for a better tomorrow

The Conscious Poets

Now Available
www.innerchildpress.com

Inner Child Press Anthologies

Now Available
www.innerchildpress.com

Inner Child Press Anthologies

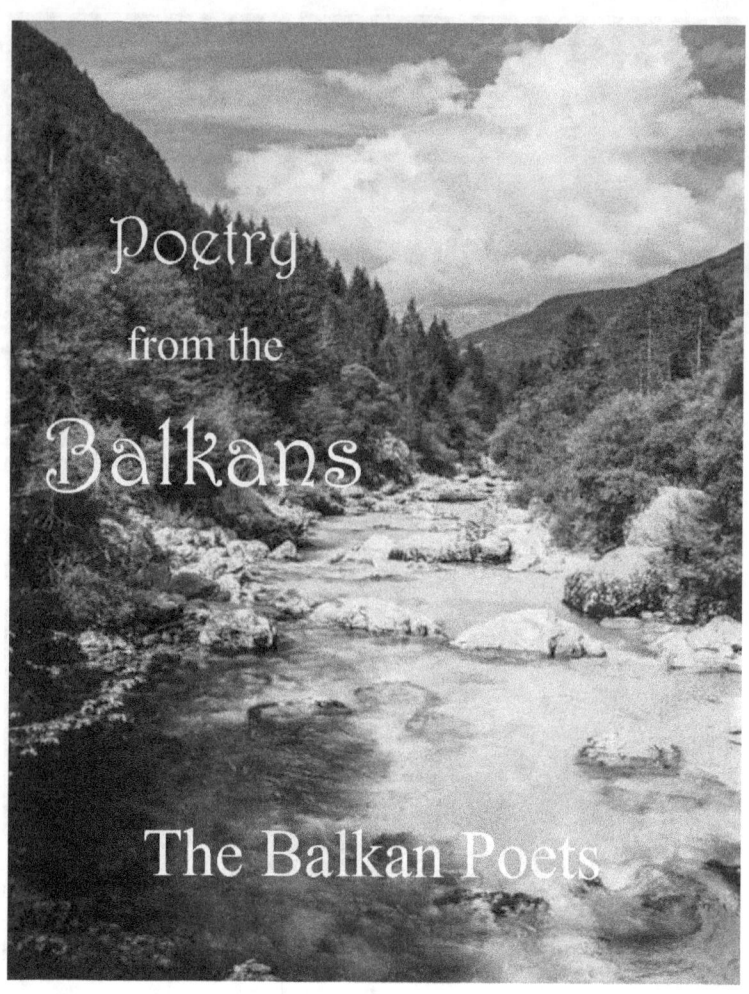

Now Available at
www.innerchildpress.com

Inner Child Press Anthologies

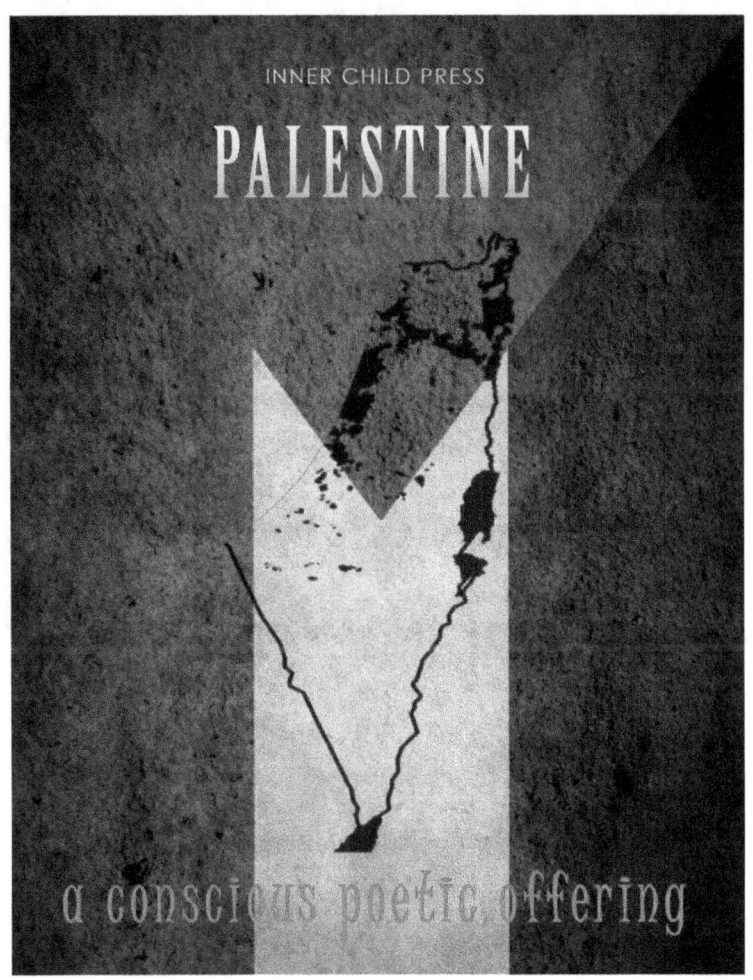

Now Available at
www.innerchildpress.com

Inner Child Press Anthologies

Now Available at
www.innerchildpress.com

Inner Child Press Anthologies

Inner Child Press International
presents

A Love Anthology
2019

The Love Poets

Now Available

www.worldhealingworldpeacepoetry.com

Inner Child Press Anthologies

Now Available

www.worldhealingworldpeacepoetry.com

Inner Child Press Anthologies

Now Available

www.worldhealingworldpeacepoetry.com

Inner Child Press Anthologies

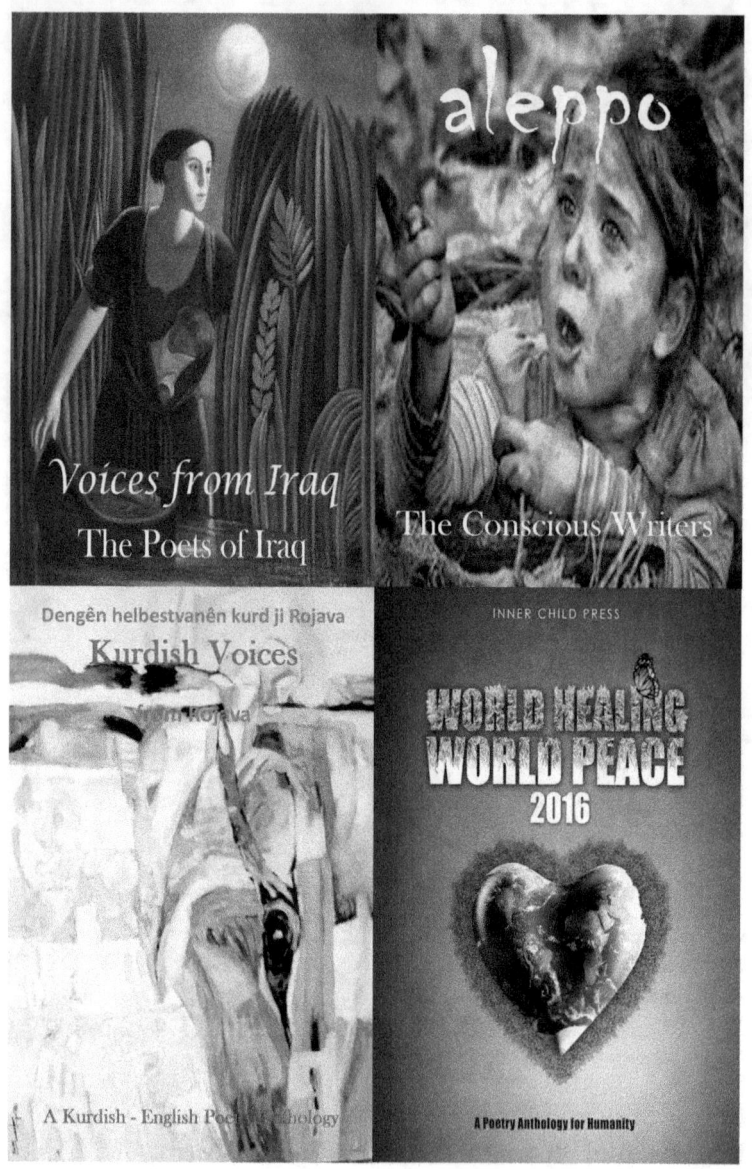

Now Available

www.innerchildpress.com/anthologies

Inner Child Press Anthologies

Now Available

www.innerchildpress.com/anthologies

Inner Child Press Anthologies

Now Available

www.innerchildpress.com/anthologies

Inner Child Press Anthologies

Now Available

www.innerchildpress.com/anthologies

Inner Child Press Anthologies

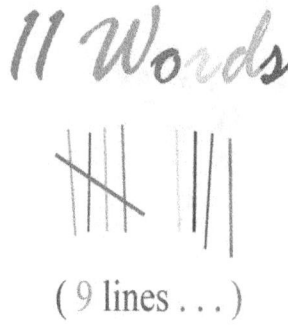

Now Available

www.innerchildpress.com/anthologies

Inner Child Press Anthologies

Now Available

www.innerchildpress.com/the-year-of-the-poet

Inner Child Press Anthologies

Now Available

www.innerchildpress.com/the-year-of-the-poet

Inner Child Press Anthologies

Now Available

www.innerchildpress.com/the-year-of-the-poet

Inner Child Press Anthologies

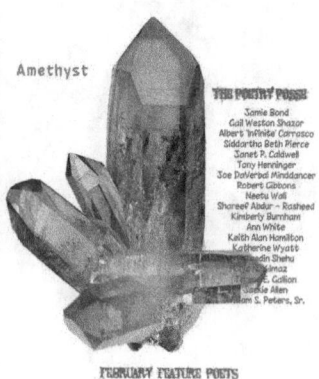

Now Available

www.innerchildpress.com/the-year-of-the-poet

Inner Child Press Anthologies

The Year of the Poet II
May 2015

May's Featured Poets
Geri Algeri
Akin Mosi Chinnery
Anna Jakubczak

Emeralds

The Poetry Posse 2015
Jamie Bond * Gail Weston Shazor * Albert 'Infinite' Carrasco
Siddartha Beth Pierce * Janet P. Caldwell * Tony Henninger
Joe DaVerbal Minddancer * Neetu Wali * Shareef Abdur – Rasheed
Kimberly Burnham * Ann White * Keith Alan Hamilton
Katherine Wyatt * Fahredin Shehu * Hülya N. Yılmaz
Teresa E. Gallion * Jackie Allen * William S. Peters, Sr.

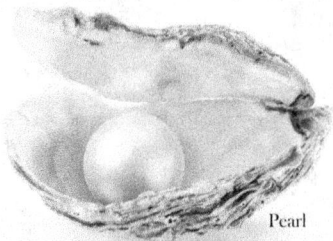

The Year of the Poet II
June 2015

June's Featured Poets
Anahit Arustamyan * Yvette D. Murrell * Regina A. Walker

Pearl

The Poetry Posse 2015
Jamie Bond * Gail Weston Shazor * Albert 'Infinite' Carrasco
Siddartha Beth Pierce * Janet P. Caldwell * Tony Henninger
Joe DaVerbal Minddancer * Neetu Wali * Shareef Abdur – Rasheed
Kimberly Burnham * Ann White * Keith Alan Hamilton
Katherine Wyatt * Fahredin Shehu * Hülya N. Yılmaz
Teresa E. Gallion * Jackie Allen * William S. Peters, Sr.

The Year of the Poet II
July 2015

The Featured Poets for July 2015
Abhik Shome * Christina Neal * Robert Neal

Rubies

The Poetry Posse 2015
Jamie Bond * Gail Weston Shazor * Albert 'Infinite' Carrasco
Siddartha Beth Pierce * Janet P. Caldwell * Tony Henninger
Joe DaVerbal Minddancer * Neetu Wali * Shareef Abdur – Rasheed
Kimberly Burnham * Ann White * Keith Alan Hamilton
Katherine Wyatt * Fahredin Shehu * Hülya N. Yılmaz
Teresa E. Gallion * Jackie Allen * William S. Peters, Sr.

The Year of the Poet II
August 2015

Peridot

Featured Poets
Gayle Howell
Ann Chalasz
Christopher Schultz

The Poetry Posse 2015
Jamie Bond * Gail Weston Shazor * Albert 'Infinite' Carrasco
Siddartha Beth Pierce * Janet P. Caldwell * Tony Henninger
Joe DaVerbal Minddancer * Neetu Wali * Shareef Abdur – Rasheed
Kimberly Burnham * Ann White * Keith Alan Hamilton
Katherine Wyatt * Fahredin Shehu * Hülya N. Yılmaz
Teresa E. Gallion * Jackie Allen * William S. Peters, Sr.

Now Available

www.innerchildpress.com/the-year-of-the-poet

Inner Child Press Anthologies

Now Available

www.innerchildpress.com/the-year-of-the-poet

Now Available

www.innerchildpress.com/the-year-of-the-poet

Inner Child Press Anthologies

Now Available

www.innerchildpress.com/the-year-of-the-poet

Inner Child Press Anthologies

Now Available

www.innerchildpress.com/the-year-of-the-poet

Inner Child Press Anthologies

Now Available

www.innerchildpress.com/the-year-of-the-poet

Inner Child Press Anthologies

Now Available

www.innerchildpress.com/the-year-of-the-poet

Inner Child Press Anthologies

The Year of the Poet IV
September 2017

Featured Poets
Martina Reisz Newberry
Ameer Nassir
Christine Fulco Neal
Robert Neal

The Elm Tree

The Poetry Posse 2017

Gail Weston Shazor * Caroline Nazareno * Bismay Mohanty
Teresa E. Gallion * Anna Jakubczak Vel Ratty Adalan
Joe DaVerbal Minddancer * Shareef Abdur – Rasheed
Albert Carrasco * Kimberly Burnham * Elizabeth Castillo
Hülya N. Yılmaz * Faleeha Hassan * Jackie Davis Allen
Jen Walls * Nizar Sartawi * * William S. Peters, Sr.

The Year of the Poet IV
October 2017

Featured Poets
Ahmed Abu Saleem
Nedal Al-Qaeim
Sadeddin Shahin

The Black Walnut Tree

The Poetry Posse 2017

Gail Weston Shazor * Caroline Nazareno * Bismay Mohanty
Teresa E. Gallion * Anna Jakubczak Vel Ratty Adalan
Joe DaVerbal Minddancer * Shareef Abdur – Rasheed
Albert Carrasco * Kimberly Burnham * Elizabeth Castillo
Hülya N. Yılmaz * Faleeha Hassan * Jackie Davis Allen
Jen Walls * Nizar Sartawi * * William S. Peters, Sr.

The Year of the Poet IV
November 2017

Featured Poets
Kay Peters
Alfreda D. Ghee
Gabriella Garofalo
Rosemary Cappello

The Tree of Life

The Poetry Posse 2017

Gail Weston Shazor * Caroline Nazareno * Bismay Mohanty
Teresa E. Gallion * Anna Jakubczak Vel Ratty Adalan
Joe DaVerbal Minddancer * Shareef Abdur – Rasheed
Albert Carrasco * Kimberly Burnham * Elizabeth Castillo
Hülya N. Yılmaz * Faleeha Hassan * Jackie Davis Allen
Jen Walls * Nizar Sartawi * William S. Peters, Sr.

The Year of the Poet IV
December 2017

Featured Poets
Justice Clarke
Mariel M. Pabron
Kiley Brown

The Fig Tree

The Poetry Posse 2017

Gail Weston Shazor * Caroline Nazareno * Bismay Mohanty
Teresa E. Gallion * Anna Jakubczak Vel Ratty Adalan
Joe DaVerbal Minddancer * Shareef Abdur – Rasheed
Albert Carrasco * Kimberly Burnham * Elizabeth Castillo
Hülya N. Yılmaz * Faleeha Hassan * Jackie Davis Allen
Jen Walls * Nizar Sartawi * William S. Peters, Sr.

Now Available

www.innerchildpress.com/the-year-of-the-poet

Inner Child Press Anthologies

Now Available

www.innerchildpress.com/the-year-of-the-poet

Inner Child Press Anthologies

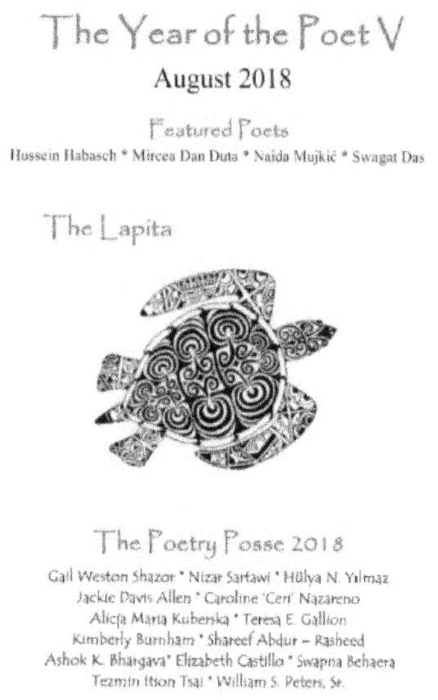

Now Available

www.innerchildpress.com/the-year-of-the-poet

Inner Child Press Anthologies

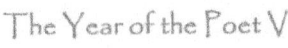

Now Available

www.innerchildpress.com/the-year-of-the-poet

Inner Child Press Anthologies

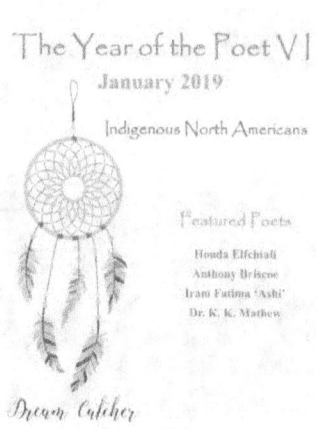

The Year of the Poet VI
January 2019

Indigenous North Americans

Featured Poets
Houda Elfchtali
Anthony Brisene
Irani Fatima 'Ashi'
Dr. K. K. Mathew

Dream Catcher

The Poetry Posse 2019

Gail Weston Shazor * Joe Paire * Hülya N. Yalmaz
Jackie Davis Allen * Caroline 'Ceri' Nazareno
Alicja Maria Kuberska * Teresa E. Gallion
Kimberly Burnham * Shareef Abdur – Rasheed
Ashok K. Bhargava * Elizabeth Castillo * Swapna Behera
Tezmin Ition Tsai * William S. Peters, Sr.

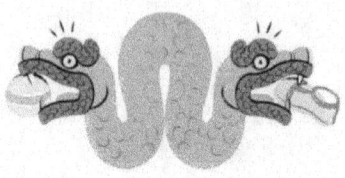

The Year of the Poet VI
February 2019

Featured Poets
Marek Lukaszewicz * Bharati Nayak
Aida G. Roque * Jean-Jacques Fournier

Meso-America

The Poetry Posse 2019

Gail Weston Shazor * Albert Carrasco * Hülya N. Yalmaz
Jackie Davis Allen * Caroline Nazareno * Eliza Segiet
Alicja Maria Kuberska * Teresa E. Gallion * Joe Paire
Kimberly Burnham * Shareef Abdur – Rasheed
Ashok K. Bhargava * Elizabeth Castillo * Swapna Behera
Tezmin Ition Tsai * William S. Peters, Sr.

The Year of the Poet VI
March 2019

Featured Poets
Eniesa Malume * Sylwia K. Malinowska
Shorouk Hammoud * Anwer Ghani

The Caribbean

The Poetry Posse 2019

Gail Weston Shazor * Albert Carrasco * Hülya N. Yalmaz
Jackie Davis Allen * Caroline Nazareno * Eliza Segiet
Alicja Maria Kuberska * Teresa E. Gallion * Joe Paire
Kimberly Burnham * Shareef Abdur – Rasheed
Ashok K. Bhargava * Elizabeth Castillo * Swapna Behera
Tezmin Ition Tsai * William S. Peters, Sr.

The Year of the Poet VI
April 2019

Featured Poets
DL Davis * Michelle Joan Barulich
Lulëzim Haziri * Faleeha Hassan

Central & West Africa

The Poetry Posse 2019

Gail Weston Shazor * Albert Carrasco * Hülya N. Yalmaz
Jackie Davis Allen * Caroline Nazareno * Eliza Segiet
Alicja Maria Kuberska * Teresa E. Gallion * Joe Paire
Kimberly Burnham * Shareef Abdur – Rasheed
Ashok K. Bhargava * Elizabeth Castillo * Swapna Behera
Tezmin Ition Tsai * William S. Peters, Sr.

Now Available

www.innerchildpress.com/the-year-of-the-poet

Inner Child Press Anthologies

Now Available

www.innerchildpress.com/the-year-of-the-poet

Inner Child Press Anthologies

Now Available

www.innerchildpress.com/the-year-of-the-poet

Inner Child Press Anthologies

The Year of the Poet VII
January 2020

Featured Poets
B S Tyagi * Ashok Chakravarthy Tholana
Andy Scott * Anwer Ghani

1901 Jean Henry Dunant and Frédéric Passy

The Year of Peace
Celebrating past Nobel Peace Prize Recipients

The Poetry Posse 2020

Gail Weston Shazor * Albert Carasco * Hülya N. Yılmaz
Jackie Davis Allen * Caroline Nazareno * Eliza Segiet
Alicja Maria Kuberska * Teresa E. Gallion * Joe Paire
Kimberly Burnham * Shareef Abdur – Rasheed
Ashok K. Bhargava * Elizabeth Castillo * Swapna Behera
Tezmin Ition Tsai * William S. Peters, Sr.

The Year of the Poet VII
February 2020

Featured Poets
Jennifer Adex * Martina Reisz Newberry
Ibrahim Honjo * Claudia Piccinno

Henri La Fontaine ~ 1913

The Year of Peace
Celebrating past Nobel Peace Prize Recipients

The Poetry Posse 2020

Gail Weston Shazor * Albert Carasco * Hülya N. Yılmaz
Jackie Davis Allen * Caroline Nazareno * Eliza Segiet
Alicja Maria Kuberska * Teresa E. Gallion * Joe Paire
Kimberly Burnham * Shareef Abdur – Rasheed
Ashok K. Bhargava * Elizabeth Castillo * Swapna Behera
Tezmin Ition Tsai * William S. Peters, Sr.

The Year of the Poet VII
March 2020

Featured Poets
Aziz Mountassir * Krishna Puraisa
Hannie Rouweler * Rozalia Aleksandrova

Aristide Briand ~ 1926 ~ Gustav Stresemann

The Year of Peace
Celebrating past Nobel Peace Prize Recipients

The Poetry Posse 2020

Gail Weston Shazor * Albert Carasco * Hülya N. Yılmaz
Jackie Davis Allen * Caroline Nazareno * Eliza Segiet
Alicja Maria Kuberska * Teresa E. Gallion * Joe Paire
Kimberly Burnham * Shareef Abdur – Rasheed
Ashok K. Bhargava * Elizabeth Castillo * Swapna Behera
Tezmin Ition Tsai * William S. Peters, Sr.

The Year of the Poet VII
April 2020

Featured Poets
Rohini Behera * Mircea Dan Duta
Monalisa Dash Dwibedy * NilavroNill Shouvro

Carlos Saavedra Lamas ~ 1936

The Year of Peace
Celebrating past Nobel Peace Prize Recipients

The Poetry Posse 2020

Gail Weston Shazor * Albert Carasco * Hülya N. Yılmaz
Jackie Davis Allen * Caroline Nazareno * Eliza Segiet
Alicja Maria Kuberska * Teresa E. Gallion * Joe Paire
Kimberly Burnham * Shareef Abdur – Rasheed
Ashok K. Bhargava * Elizabeth Castillo * Swapna Behera
Tezmin Ition Tsai * William S. Peters, Sr.

Now Available

www.innerchildpress.com/the-year-of-the-poet

Inner Child Press Anthologies

Now Available

www.innerchildpress.com/the-year-of-the-poet

Inner Child Press Anthologies

Now Available

www.innerchildpress.com/the-year-of-the-poet

Inner Child Press Anthologies

The Year of the Poet VIII
January 2021

Featured Global Poets
Andrew Scott • Debaprasanna Biswas
Shakil Kalam • Changming Yuan

Banksy's The Girl with the Pierced Eardrum

Poetry ... Ekphrasticly Speaking
The Poetry Posse 2020

Gail Weston Shazor • Albert Carasco • Hülya N. Yılmaz
Jackie Davis Allen • Caroline Nazareno • Eliza Segiet
Alicja Maria Kuberska • Teresa E. Gallion • Joe Paire
Kimberly Burnham • Shareef Abdur – Rasheed
Ashok K. Bhargava • Elizabeth Castillo • Swapna Behera
Tezmin Ition Tsai • William S. Peters, Sr.

The Year of the Poet VIII
February 2021

Featured Global Poets
T. Ramesh Babu • Ruchida Barman
Neptune Barman • Faleeha Hassan

Emory Douglas : 1968 Olympics mural

Poetry ... Ekphrasticly Speaking
The Poetry Posse 2021

Gail Weston Shazor • Albert Carasco • Hülya N. Yılmaz
Jackie Davis Allen • Caroline Nazareno • Eliza Segiet
Alicja Maria Kuberska • Teresa E. Gallion • Joe Paire
Kimberly Burnham • Shareef Abdur – Rasheed
Ashok K. Bhargava • Elizabeth Castillo • Swapna Behera
Tezmin Ition Tsai • William S. Peters, Sr.

The Year of the Poet VIII
March 2021

Featured Global Poets
Claudia Piccinno • Mohammed Jabr
Luzviminda Rivera • Nigar Arif

Tatyana Fazlalizadeh

Poetry ... Ekphrasticly Speaking
The Poetry Posse 2021

Gail Weston Shazor • Albert Carasco • Hülya N. Yılmaz
Jackie Davis Allen • Caroline Nazareno • Eliza Segiet
Alicja Maria Kuberska • Teresa E. Gallion • Joe Paire
Kimberly Burnham • Shareef Abdur – Rasheed
Ashok K. Bhargava • Elizabeth Castillo • Swapna Behera
Tezmin Ition Tsai • William S. Peters, Sr.

The Year of the Poet VIII
April 2021

Featured Global Poets
Katarzyna Brus-Sawczuk • Anwesha Paul
Rozalia Aleksandrova • Shahid Abbas

Pablo O'Higgins

Poetry ... Ekphrasticly Speaking
The Poetry Posse 2021

Gail Weston Shazor • Albert Carasco • Hülya N. Yılmaz
Jackie Davis Allen • Caroline Nazareno • Eliza Segiet
Alicja Maria Kuberska • Teresa E. Gallion • Joe Paire
Kimberly Burnham • Shareef Abdur – Rasheed
Ashok K. Bhargava • Elizabeth Castillo • Swapna Behera
Tezmin Ition Tsai • William S. Peters, Sr.

Now Available

www.innerchildpress.com/the-year-of-the-poet

Inner Child Press Anthologies

Now Available

www.innerchildpress.com/the-year-of-the-poet

and there is much, much more !

visit . . .

www.innerchildpress.com/anthologies-sales-special.php

Also check out our Authors and all the wonderful Books Available at :

www.innerchildpress.com/authors-pages

World Healing World Peace 2020

Poets for Humanity

Now Available

www.worldhealingworldpeacepoetry.com

Now Available

www.worldhealingworldpeacepoetry.com

World Healing World Peace
2012, 2014, 2016, 2018, 2020

Now Available

www.worldhealingworldpeacepoetry.com

Inner Child Press International

'building bridges of cultural understanding'

Meet the Board of Directors

William S. Peters, Sr.
Chair Person
Founder
Inner Child Enterprises
Inner Child Press

Hülya N Yılmaz
Director
Editing Services
Co-Chair Person

Fahredin B. Shehu
Director
Cultural Affairs

Elizabeth E. Castillo
Director
Recording Secretary

De'Andre Hawthorne
Director
Performance Poetry

Gail Weston Shazor
Director
Anthologies

Kimberly Burnham
Director
Cultural Ambassador
Pacific Northwest
USA

Ashok K. Bhargava
Director
WIN Awards

Deborah Smart
Director
Publicity
Marketing

www.innerchildpress.com

Inner Child Press International
'building bridges of cultural understanding'
Meet our Cultural Ambassadors

Fahredin Shehu
Director of Cultural

Faleeha Hassan
Iraq – USA

Elizabeth E. Castillo
Philippines

Antoinette Coleman
Chicago
Midwest USA

Ananda Nepali
Nepal – Tibet
Northern India

Kimberly Burnham
Pacific Northwest
USA

Alicja Kuberska
Poland
Eastern Europe

Swapna Behera
India
Southeast Asia

Kolade O. Freedom
Nigeria
West Africa

Mansif Beroual
Morocco
Northern Africa

Ashok K. Bhargava
Canada

Tzemin Ition Tsai
Republic of China
Greater China

Alicia M. Ramírez
Mexico
Central America

Christena AV Williams
Jamaica
Caribbean

Louise Hudon
Eastern Canada

Aziz Mountassir
Morocco
Northern Africa

Shareef Abdur-Rasheed
Southeastern USA

Laure Charazac
France
Western Europe

Mohammad Iqbal Harb
Lebanon
Middle East

Mohamed Abdel
Aziz Shmeis
Egypt
Middle East

Hilary Mainga
Kenya
Eastern Africa

Josephus R. Johnson
Liberia

www.innerchildpress.com

This Anthological Publication
is underwritten solely by

Inner Child Press International

Inner Child Press is a Publishing Company Founded and Operated by Writers. Our personal publishing experiences provides us an intimate understanding of the sometimes daunting challenges Writers, New and Seasoned may face in the Business of Publishing and Marketing their Creative "Written Work".

For more Information

Inner Child Press International

www.innerchildpress.com

building bridges of cultural understanding
202 Wiltree Court, State College, Pennsylvania 16801

www.innerchildpress.com

~ fini ~

www.ingramcontent.com/pod-product-compliance
Lightning Source LLC
LaVergne TN
LVHW022322080426
835508LV00041B/1693